BOMBS AND BLACKBERRIES

BOMBS AND BLACKBERRIES

A CHIILDHOOD IN BRENCHLEY FROM 1927 ONWARDS

BY

NORA VEYSEY

Date of Publication
(October 1996)

Published by CHICA

© Nora Veysey

Printed by:
ProPrint
Riverside Cottage
Great North Road
Stibbington
Peterborough PE8 6LR

ISBN 0 9528992 0 5

CONTENTS

Page No.

INTRODUCTION

I began writing my memories of my childhood in pre-war and wartime Kent so that my daughter could have a record of the happenings and events of that time. I wanted her to know what it was that made me the person that I am today, and also to understand what village life was like in the years before cars were a necessity, when telephones were only for the rich and television, as we know it, was many years away.

As I wrote, I found that memories came flooding back, until the work grew into a book, and led me on, beyond the war years, to 1947. Those of my friends who have been given the opportunity to read it have encouraged me to make it available to a wider audience.

I hope you will enjoy reading it as much as I have enjoyed writing it.

FOR PAULA

CHAPTER 1

Out of school - across the road and through the gate into the blackberry field called the Rayments we went. I never knew why it had such a name - or even how to spell it - Raiments, Raymence, Ramence. I suspect it was a field belonging to a family called Rayment so it was the Rayment's field, just as there was Peter's field further along the road. Anyway, that was the route we took after school to go and find Mum on the farm. It was a mile from one end of the farm to the other and we went in somewhere in the middle of it. We usually knew where she would be.

'Come straight up to the logans in Number 18,' we would be told before she left in the morning, or 'Number 16 tonight - raspberries.'

There was quite a gang of us trailing along every day and we quite enjoyed the trip along the farm track. At one point, a stream went under the track and the ground around it was soft, marshy and wooded. We hurried over that bit as we thought it rather sinister. One afternoon there was a dragon-fly there and we were scared to go by. We waited for ages for it to go away but it didn't. We believed it had a sting worse than fifty wasps so we felt very brave as, one by one, we dashed past. Our mums were getting anxious by this time so we were all in trouble for dawdling.

Cherry picking time was best. We took a different route then - out of school, along the road past the hall and then across a field and through a gap in the hedge and we were in the cherry orchard. We had a two week holiday from school during cherry picking time - end of June, beginning of July - because the main holiday didn't begin till the third week in August and lasted till the first week in October. That was the hop-picking holiday.

The cherry orchard had all its long grass and weeds cut down before picking began, so we always made huge nests and sat in them munching cherries. If I never have another cherry in my life I've had my share. Remembering those days in the orchard, I cannot bring myself to pay over a pound for cherries now.

To scare the birds away from the fruit there were sheets of galvanised iron fastened on to six or seven trees around the orchard. By pulling a string, the

1

cherry minder could lift hefty pieces of scrap iron and let them bang back on to those sheets. Three or four crashes of this contraption should have scared every bird within a mile radius at least.

The cherry minder had a green tarpaulin tent somewhere central in the orchard and all the strings led to the tent. He would sit there on an upturned apple box, puffing on his pipe, pulling the strings every few minutes and yelling at kids in between. Sometimes he left his tent and went round the orchard with his gun - taking pot shots at any birds he could see. The boys used to collect the empty cartridges - heaven only knows what for. Sometimes he hung up one of his victims as a grim reminder to its kind. I don't know what these carcasses did to the birds but they certainly scared me.

Cherries have never tasted the same since those days. We hung around under the ladders feasting on the ones that dropped from the pickers' hands. Our own mums would make sure that some good ones fell for us.

'I would like three boxes of your very best cherries.' said a la-di-dah visitor to the boss one day as they walked round inspecting the trees.
'I can let you have some very good cherries' was the reply, 'but the best ones are eaten by the ladies as they pick.'

One year, when I was very small, there were chickens in the orchard and so there were grains of maize all over the place, pretty, triangular, orange things and for no reason that I can think of I put one up my nose - which began to bleed. I couldn't get it out and started crying. Someone fetched my mum and all hell broke loose. I was scared I would be in trouble for misuse of a grain of maize - that's why I was crying. As usual, Mum rose to the occasion and got it out.

Next to the cherry orchard was a patch of rough ground with an evil smelling ditch running through it. It was fenced off because it didn't belong to the farm, but the spiles of the fence were old and some of them were missing, so it was quite easy for us children to squeeze through the gaps. We didn't like it in there very much but on the other side of the ditch were two or three pear trees of a variety not to be found anywhere else on the farm. I don't know what they were but they were small and sweet and we loved them.

Mum worked from 8 till 5 and, schooldays or holidays, at 4.30 we were sent home. It was our job to light the fire in the kitchen range, set the table ready for tea and have a kettle boiling by the time Mum got home.

Early on in her career on the farm, my Mum was advised by a mate,
'Take my tip, say you'll be a ladder worker. You can earn more.'
'But I'm terrified of heights.'
'So was I when I started. You'll get used to it - you'll get used to anything if it pays well enough.'

And she did. Like me, she hated hops and hop-picking and was very happy to spend the hop-picking season up a ladder picking apples.

We ate apples till we looked like them and always took a few home in our bags and pockets. We were never short of fruit then. One particular day, when we had been sent home, we chose to walk through one of the apple orchards. I saw a very dainty-looking tree absolutely loaded with apples and there were lots on the grass underneath it as well. I picked one up to try it and found it to be the most delicious apple I had ever tasted, so I picked up a few to take home for Mum. My pocket seemed to hold more than I expected and I found there was a large hole in my pocket and all the apples were falling down into the lining. I collected as many as I could and took off my coat and carried it because it was uncomfortable to have all those apples bumping round my legs. When I got them home, they filled a huge bowl and I showed them to Mum with great pride.
'They taste every so nice, Mum' I told her.
'I'm not surprised' she said, 'they're best Cox's.'
Cox's are still my favourite apples.

Apple orchards were situated all over the farm, so we never knew where she might be, but there was always someone to ask. One orchard was on a wicked slope and two rather hefty ladies had put their ladders in a tree from opposite sides and locked them together at the top thinking this was an extra safety measure. As they reached the top of their 20 stave ladders, they began to tip sideways and fell right out of the tree. How the ladies escaped with only cuts and bruises I'll never know.

We weren't too happy if Mum was in the nut orchard. True, it contained lots of trees of Miller apples - gorgeous, sweet and crisp when barely ripe, - and the cobnuts and filberts were toothsome too, but it also contained a flock of geese. Vicious creatures those geese were. They came at us with their necks stretched out and their beaks wide open, hissing like a cave full of dragons. We were terrified of them and not even the Millers would tempt us in unless the geese were at the other end of the orchard.

Plums needed ladder-workers too. Mum was picking plums when the Battle of Britain raged overhead - and we all had gas-masks in the field with us. One day, early in the war, a convoy of Canadians got lost in the narrow country lanes and stopped by the plum orchard while they sorted themselves out. Basketful after basketful of plums were emptied into their lorries and jeeps. The ladies' earnings were low that day and the farmer never knew how many plums he lost.

There were fields of blackcurrant bushes - well, to be honest, they were really blackberry fields with blackcurrants planted in the 'bays' between the blackberry canes. Mum quite enjoyed picking currants because it was a job you could sit down to. The ladies carried a half-bushel apple box from bush to bush and were expert at clearing a bush without moving the box. I liked picking blackcurrants too, I don't know why, but I never needed to be forced into helping Mum when she was in the blackcurrants.

There was a strawberry field too, but Mum avoided picking strawberries if she could because she had a chronically bad back and suffered agonies if she had to bend down too much. We felt a bit ill-used over this as strawberries were luxury fruit, but we didn't fare too badly as we often had to pass the strawberry field on our way to find Mum and, like as not, there was no-one in it to witness our scrumping.

The crown of the year for all of us was when the blackberries were ripe. There were four huge fields of blackberries - Church Field, Number Five, Number Six and the Rayments. It was like painting the Forth Bridge, as soon as the fourth field had been picked the first one was ready again. The blackberries were ripe during the hop-picking holiday and we children were expected to do our share and help to earn the cost of our winter clothes.

The blackberry canes were trained on rows of wire that stretched from one side of the field to the other with a track either end. Somewhere in the middle of the field - by the track, was the inevitable green tarpaulin tent, the weighing-up tent, presided over by two dragons, the foreman's wife and her mate. In the tent were piles of empty fruit baskets - chips we called them - of the size we were to use that day, 2lb, 4lb or 6lb. It took a lot of picking to fill a 6lb chip. Each person collected six or seven chips and threaded a length of stout string through the handles - if you were an old hand you had a leather belt - then you tied the string round your waist with all the chips bunched up round you. You pulled one to the front of you and you were ready for the off. That way you had both hands free for picking.

The rows were allocated in strict rotation - one row per person, or family, or couple if you wanted to work in twos. Mum and her workmate, Mrs. Brooker, known to everyone just as Brooker, always kept together and whoever finished their row first helped the other one. As Mum had three children picking for her, usually one of us worked on Brooker's row. As you filled your chips they were left under a cane and at intervals were taken up and piled up at the end of the row. When the day or the row or the session was finished, we carried the chips to the weighing-up tent and left them there in a named pile to be dealt with by the dragons. They were weighed and the totals entered in your 'book.' There was an art to carrying those chips - three in each hand. You put your index and middle fingers through the handles of two chips and with your thumb you held the third one on top, crosswise.

The day began at 8 o'clock. When we were in Church Field, the church clock was easily seen and at 9.15 we had lunch - a sandwich or two and a cup of tea from flasks filled before we left home. Midday was dinner time, when Mum and Brooker made a fire from brushwood and boiled the kettle. It was a billy can really. When it boiled, they put some tea in it and there was enough for us and to fill the flasks for the afternoon. We had an hour for dinner and we hastily swallowed our food - sandwiches with jam or paste or cheese, a packet of crisps, a piece of plain cake or a biscuit - not too much, nothing fancy. I've never liked picnics since, I had enough of them. Then we were free to play. Actually, Mum used to give us some play time during the afternoon if we'd worked hard. We would go into the wagon lodge and play chase among the wagons and carts - though the farmer put a stop to that - miserable old so and so. Sometimes there was hay to play on or we would go into the apple orchard and make a camp out of the boxes that had been piled up ready for the apple-picking. At other times, we scrambled among the hedges finding wild hazel nuts, or we just sat around and played in the dirt.

There was one time when an unheard of thing happened and Mum left work after we had had our dinner because she had to go to London with Pop - something to do with the fish business he was running , I think. She left us with Brooker and told us to go on picking and earn as much as we could. Brooker was a hard taskmaster and made sure that we didn't slack. We took our full baskets up to the tent and left them in a neat pile with our name on them in the accepted manner. When we came back with the next lot, our pile had vanished and somebody else had got fruit where ours had been. Brooker had much to say about it.
'Those little kids have worked hard all the afternoon' she said. 'They wanted to surprise their Mum, and now someone has nicked all their fruit.' She said it over and over again to anyone who would listen, but it didn't make any difference, the fruit had gone.

Most of the blackberry fields had a primitive loo tucked away in a corner somewhere, just a rough wooden hut with a wooden seat incorporating a suitably sized hole over a fairly deep pit. One morning, when we were working in the Rayments, my two sisters and I trotted off to the loo and we all went in together which was a pretty tight squeeze. When we were ready to come out, we couldn't open the door. We pulled and tugged separately and together. We checked the latch and the bolt on the door but it was no use. We could not open the door. So we did the only thing there was left for us to do - we yelled. It seemed that no-one was going to take any notice of us at all, so we yelled louder than ever. Back in the field people began to be aware of the noise and asked each other what they thought it was.
'Sounds like kids,' said someone.
'Where are your kids, Lucy?' said Brooker, 'I haven't seen them for some time.'
'You're right,' said Mum and the two of them followed the noise. They pulled open the door and we tumbled out.

6

'We couldn't get out Mum,' we said, expecting sympathy. 'The door was stuck. We pulled and pulled and we couldn't open it.'

'I'm not surprised,' she answered. 'Did you try pushing it? It opens outwards.' She wasn't pleased. We had to pick longer that day to make up for the time she'd lost coming to rescue us.

If the field didn't have a loo in it, one had to slip off discreetly to the end of the row where one had to select a suitable spot avoiding nettles, thistles and blackberry thorns and hope that no-one came by. Often dock leaves served as loo paper and everything was carefully buried under a mound of 'clads,' big lumps of soil that had been left when the tractor had come through earlier in the year to plough in the weeds.

During the blackberry season, our hands were permanently stained with juice. Nothing really shifted it although we tried pumice stone, various proprietary soaps and bleach. We also had the problem of thorns - our hands were never free from them and we all became expert at removing them from each other. Wasps were a hazard too and we were frequently stung.

When the last berries had been picked, the summer workers were laid off and only the regulars remained to clear the last remaining apples. Then it was time to tie up the blackberries, cut off the old wood and tie the healthy new canes on to the wire. There were apples and pears to be packed, neatly arranged in layers in bushel baskets, and other jobs too, at various times through the winter. Root crops, such as swedes, would be stored in huge 'clamps.' These were long, wide, shallow trenches into which the roots would be tipped and then covered up with earth, making a shape like a prehistoric barrow. The clamp would be opened a little at a time and the ladies would have to take out the roots and inspect them, discarding any suspect ones and packing the good ones into boxes to be sent to market. That was cold work. We didn't enjoy going to the farm to find Mum on those bleak, late autumn days, although it wasn't so bad if she was working in the oast house packing apples as she did sometimes. Then there were things to climb over and into and marvellous places to play hide-and-seek. All the seasonal workers had been stood off and there were only a few of us there to play and we were all more or less friends. Still, more often than not, we went straight home after school and waited for Mum to come. She didn't have to work quite so late as she did in the summer and came home at half past four.

Mum's employment on the farm ended one day during the war. The foreman - known by one and all as Old Beadle - came through the field where the ladies were working, calling out various names, including Mum's and Brookers'. When they went to find out why they were wanted,they were told that they were to go to another farm some two miles away where there was work to be done. Mum flatly refused to go.

'I can't do that,' she said. 'My children will be coming to find me when they leave school. What are they going to do if I'm not here?'

'Somebody will tell them where you are,' said Beadle.

'And then what will they do?' she retorted. 'Walk the two miles along the main road to find me. There are plenty of women who haven't been called. Why do you choose one with children?'

'I chose people who have bicycles,' he said.

'I have my bicycle for my own convenience, not yours,' she said. 'There is plenty of work here. Why can't I go back to what I was doing?'

'You needn't think you are going to pick your own jobs.' he blustered, and for the rest of that day, Mum and Brooker - who had backed Mum all the way - were sent to work in the nut orchard, well away from the other women. I suppose he thought they were a bad influence.

The next morning when they reported for work, they were kept waiting around in the farmyard while everyone else started work.

At last, Mum said to Beadle,

'Either you find me some work to do or give me my cards. I have plenty of things I could be doing at home and I don't intend to waste my time sitting here.'

In hindsight I can appreciate his dilemma. Mum and Brooker were good friends of his wife and he could foresee trouble at home. They were also his two most valuable workers, but he felt he had a point to make and his credibility was at stake. He gave them their cards.

From then on Mum went back to housework - charring. She worked mornings only, she no longer had to brave the weather and she could work the whole year round. Her 'ladies' treated her very well and were very good to us children.

Some time later her contacts on the farm reported a sharp exchange of words between the 'ladder mover' in the apple orchard and Beadle.

'We're never going to get these apples picked at this rate,' yelled Beadle. 'What sort of people have you got up those ladders? Can't they pick any faster?'

'Don't blame me,' was the reply. 'It's entirely your own fault. You sacked your two best ladder workers. You should have thought a bit more before you did that.'

Vindication?

CHAPTER 2

During Mum's career as a farm worker, late autumn meant that work for the year had ended and Mum stayed at home. That was wonderful. We would get home from school to a warm house with a fire crackling in the grate. A dark tablecloth would be over the table and, like as not, Mum would be busy at her sewing machine. She made clothes for all of us, dresses, skirts, blouses, nighties and, for my brother, endless pairs of trousers. In those days a jumble sale produced enough material to fit out a household - very few people expected to wear the garments as they were sold, they were unpicked and made into smaller clothes. She knitted as well - jumpers and cardigans for all of us. Strangely enough, all our socks were made by our father who had somehow acquired an early kind of knitting machine. It produced a tubular garment and had an attachment for turning heels. He knitted sock after sock, each one joined to the other with a strip of knitting in cotton. Mum would then cut the cotton and finish off the toes with her knitting needles. We always had plenty of socks and they were always black. Whilst he was knitting, the little needles would be scattered all over the floor and it was our job to find them for him. He couldn't afford to lose them as they were irreplaceable. We always knew when a needle went down by the long drawn out D-A-A-A-M-N which accompanied it. My father didn't know the meaning of the word patience - or tact either come to that. He re-soled our shoes too when they needed it and then we had to crawl all over the floor picking up nails. The 'damns' came more often when he was cobbling - with extra special ones when he hit his thumb!

We spent time crawling over the floor when Uncle Frank was icing the Christmas cake too, but that was different because we were searching for the little silver balls that he used for decoration. When we found them,we ate them.

Pop left the job of disciplining us to Mum. He yelled at us often but we let that wash over us. If we really raised his temper he would hit out at whoever was nearest, so we quickly learned to keep out of reach. Mum was different. She hardly ever lost her temper and when she punished us it was done completely cold-bloodedly. She assessed the magnitude of the crime, decided on a fitting punishment and carried it out. If we ran away, it was waiting when we returned ---- plus! We knew exactly where we stood with Mum.

The fireplace in the living-room was situated across one corner of the room and the mantelpiece above it had been extended so that it had an angle. In this angle Mum kept The Stick. It stood behind a biscuit tin and leaned against the picture of Uncle Ted. It was my Dad's old army cane actually. When we transgressed badly enough Mum would say,
'Go and get my stick.' and we had to get it, give it to her, receive a couple of cuts on each hand and then put it back in its place. We knew better than to argue or try to dodge the issue in any way - two cuts could become three if we were slow in obeying.

I can remember only one instance when Mum lost her temper with any of us. It was when my elder sister, Nellie, answered one of Mum's instructions with
'Shan't for you!' as she had heard her friends do. She misjudged her timing and Mum heard her. She didn't wait for the stick but gave her a good slapping. Nellie sobbed for ages, curled up in an armchair, but she never tried it again.

As our house had once been a pub, the living room as we called it, was lined with ranks of shelves, mostly filled with clutter. On one of those shelves, always in the same place, sat the sweet tin. Pop kept it supplied, but we had to ask for a sweet if we fancied one. Mum hardly ever said no, but no way did we open that tin without asking. Sometimes it was just too much trouble to ask so we went without. I guess it was one way of making sure that we didn't ruin our teeth. We never had any pocket money of our own. One day, Mum asked me to go down to the village to buy something that she had run out of. When I got back, she asked me if I would mind going down again as there was something else she had forgotten. I didn't mind a bit, I quite enjoyed going, but she felt very guilty about it and gave me 2d to spend for myself. I felt like a millionaire!

On Saturdays, or in school holidays when Mum wasn't working, we all 'went out to play.' In fact, Mum made sure we did. We weren't allowed to play indoors unless it was wet or really cold. Indeed, sometimes we stayed outside in the rain, playing in the shed - or lodge as we called it, which was huge.

Before we were allowed out we had our regular jobs to do. Every day we had to do table setting and washing-up and emptying the 'jerries' in the bedrooms - our only loo was at the end of the garden. On Saturdays, we had to clean all the boots and shoes - the whole lot - and all the forks and spoons too. In her younger days, Mum had been a parlour-maid and she liked things to be clean and shining. Her glassware, crockery and cutlery might be cheap but it always shone. I quite enjoyed making things shine so I didn't mind getting busy with the Goddard's Plate Powder mixed up with a little meths and rubbing hard to remove as much stain as I could from the spoons. Mum also had six silver teaspoons which her 'lady' had given her as a wedding present. These were wrapped in felt and never used, so I never had the joy of cleaning them. They are mine now, and they get used and cleaned, but not with Goddard's Plate Powder. I feel really close to my Mum when I clean those spoons.

Usually, when we went out to play, we knew exactly where we were going and what we were going to do. I can't remember any discussion or argument - we just went. As far as Mum was concerned we could go wherever we liked as long as we could hear her whistle. When it was dinner or tea time, or if she needed us for any reason, she stood outside and blew her whistle - like a guard's whistle it was - and the sound really carried. We knew almost to within an inch how far away from home we dared to be.

Our favourite place was known to us as the tree trunk. About a couple of hundred yards from home was a cross-roads, on one corner of which was a really high bank. Clinging to the top of the bank was a huge oak tree. As they left the trunk, its massive roots were partly exposed, and between them and under them were little alcoves and hidey-holes. To the left of the tree was a little copse with well worn paths, hidden nooks, patches of primroses, bluebells and dog-violets and, at its edge, a murky pond with fallen branches and tree-stumps in it so that you could walk dry-shod across it if your legs were long enough and you had the courage. We would play on that tree-trunk for days at a time - schools, homes, cowboys and Indians - the possibilities were almost endless. Parents today would shudder at the danger of falling down the bank and under the wheels of a car, but cars were few and far between and none of us ever fell anyway. The tree-trunk is still there and looks exactly the same as it did sixty-odd years ago, except that the grass is cut more often and the whole place looks tidier --- but no child ever plays there.

Over the cross-roads and down a steep hill were the primrose woods. Again, there were well-worn paths and favourite nooks and crannies and also a stream. In the summer, the brambles and creepers were so rampant that we couldn't play there, but in the spring, we would emerge when we heard Mum's whistle - wet, muddy, scratched, stung with nettles, bruised, tired and thoroughly happy. We would pick primroses by the bowlful and Mum would pack them in shoe boxes and post them to her sister and friends who lived in towns. She knew they would be delivered next morning and would bring pleasure to a lot of people.

Behind the house was a hayfield where we loved to play. In the late spring and early summer, it was a treasure house of yellow buttercups, red sorrel, white 'horse-daisies' and, in one corner, bluebells and a few primroses. We played hide - and - seek there because we could lie down in the grass and be completely invisible. We went looking for bird's nests and wild blackberries. When the grass was short and not stubbly, we played rounders. Sometimes, on fine evenings, some of the grown-ups would come and play with us. Pop, Uncle Frank, Auntie Florrie and the lady from next door would come - but Mum never came, not even to watch. We loved it at first when the grown-ups joined in, but after a little while, one got a bit tired of always having to chase to the other side of the field to get the ball and never having a chance to bat.

We played rounders in the road too. There was a field gate opposite with a wide run-in and on our side of the road a gap in the railings. Our house having been a pub, this must have been the way in. Anyway, these two openings gave us our four corners for rounders. Now, it is a busy road leading to a main-line station and traffic is practically non-stop, but then, there was just an occasional car which caused us to cease operations for a few minutes - and gave us time to get our breath back. We lived right on the crest of a hill and it was nothing to have to chase the ball for almost half-a-mile, over the cross-roads and down beyond the beginnings of the primrose woods - and then drag all the way back up the hill with it. Like as not, by the time you got back, the rest of them would have found another ball and the game would have gone on in your absence, quite often losing you your turn at batting. A left-hander could send it down the other hill, almost down into the village. Our own rules wouldn't allow more than one rounder off a single hit or one good swipe could have won the game.

There were several smallish ponds within whistle distance, and I was a sucker for water. Mum used to say that if I was missing she looked for the nearest water, be it sea, stream, pond, puddle or tap. One such pond had water lilies on it - beautiful, waxy, yellow flowers. I loved them and longed to get one for Mum. I tried - I really tried, but the water was just too deep and my fingers too pudgy so I just couldn't manage it. After I'd fallen in for the third time, Mum put that pond out of bounds, but that didn't stop me. One day, with an air of great triumph, I finally presented Mum with a water-lily bloom. Looking back I can appreciate her dilemma and, to be perfectly honest, I cannot now remember whether it was the stick for disobedience or not. I can't even decide what I would have done in her place. There is a water-lily gradually unfolding right now in my own little garden pond. It is just that same waxy yellow colour and it takes me right back to the one I picked for Mum.

Our home was very near to the Jubilee Seat. Set in a semi-circle of trellised fencing and placed under a canopy of beech trees this has a commanding view over the Weald - the valley of the Medway, the Teise and the Beult - over the hills to Maidstone and beyond to Bluebell Hill. In those days, the field fell away behind the fence, and it was an easy thing for us to climb over the fence and race down into the dip, as we called the deep hollow in the nearest field.

After a long period of wet weather when we had had to stay inside, we decided to visit the dip. The grass was wet and rather muddy but we all had wellies on and so over the fence we went. We ran full pelt down the field and found to our horror that the dip was now a pond. We were utterly unable to stop and, before we realised what was happening, we were up to our knees in water. With our wellies full of water and our skirts all wet, we squelched home. Poor Mum!

Beyond the field opposite the house, was a chestnut wood. We didn't go there very often because Mr. Lawrence kept chickens in the field and his wife chased us out. Sometimes we found nests of eggs where the hens had laid astray, and at first we would dutifully take them round to her, but she only grunted - which might or might not be 'thank you' - so after that we took the eggs to Mum. There were other chestnut trees within easy reach and when the nuts were ripe we collected them by the ton. We had them boiled and roasted and made into soup - delicious in any way, but most of all, we just ate them raw. Chestnuts don't taste the same now.

Now everything has changed. All the hedges have been removed from the little fields to make one large cornfield. The primrose woods have been cleared to make the cornfield larger. The secret little stream is just a deep cleft in the field. The field opposite has been covered in little bungalows and their gardens have swallowed up the little wood by the tree-trunk. The old house has been pulled down and a modern box built there. The hayfield is built on and most of the chestnut trees have gone. Such is progress!

Half way down the hill to the village was a massive sequoia tree (pictured on the cover) - known to us all as the fir tree. It had a rickety metal fence round it on the field side and we could climb up the bank to it on the road side. It was as rotten as could be. We could all climb up a few branches and the boys went almost to the top. For the Coronation of King George V1 and Queen Elizabeth, Maury Lawrence put a Union Jack right on the top of it, so, when the war was over and Maury was due home from the army, my brother decided to repeat the tribute. The tree was even more rotten by then and he lost his nerve so the flag stuck out at the side quite a way from the top, still, like Christmas, it's the thought that counts. That tree was no trouble to anyone until houses were built in the field, then it became a danger and was felled. Pity!

When I was very young, too young to understand what was going on, we were occasionally invaded by hordes of Londoners, at least it seemed like hordes. They usually came during hop-picking and for some reason, Mum put them up. Sometimes she knew when they were coming and had time to prepare beds, but at other times they just turned up, and often there were a few extra in the party. More than once I was woken up when I was comfortably off to sleep because some of them had arrived and Mum needed our room and our beds. We were hastily put into what she called 'down beds,' namely cushions on the floor of her room. We didn't mind, it was an adventure! At one time I wondered why she did it but the answer was simple, they had wads of money which they spent like water. When they came into the country they expected to sleep rough, so when Mum prepared a room for two of them and five or six turned up, they took it in their stride.

The acknowledged leader of their group was a typical little cockney sparrow named Ernie Wood who was sometimes accompanied by his rather angular wife and sometimes not. His side kick was 'Uncle Joe.' I can't remember any other names. We quite liked them coming, as frequently the odd coin dropped in our direction or sweets or packets of crisps. Once we were taken out in their car which was a never to be forgotten experience. I don't know how many of us were packed into the thing - far more than was safe, and the driver was showing off by going much too fast. At the bottom of the hill by the primrose woods he lost control. The bends in the road there have to be treated with respect and we skidded from one side of the road to the other and back again. We ended in the ditch, unharmed but badly shaken and luckily the right way up. Mum, who alone realised the very real danger we had been in, dragooned all her family to walk back up the hill to home, while Uncle Joe kept saying,
'Don't take it badly, Missus. I didn't know he was as drunk as all that. It won't happen again.'
'Too true it won't,' said Mum. 'There'll never be the chance.'

Mum reckoned that they operated on the shady side of the law and came down to rusticate when the police got too close to them. Once, after they'd left, she found a gold watch on the wash-stand. She wrote to Ernie and told him and was asked to hold on to it till he came next time. When she duly handed it over, he told her she could keep it as his wife had a new one. It was a lovely watch and Mum wore it until she died. We never knew what happened to them but they were complete East Enders and Mum thought it was likely that they died in the bombing.

CHAPTER 3

Early in the 1930s, someone erected a huge pylon in the corner of the field by our tree-trunk. It turned out to be a beacon - for guiding aircraft, we understood. It had a huge revolving lamp on the top and, as dusk fell, the beacon lit up and the top revolved giving out a great ray of light on two sides. I know many people deplored its existence but we loved it. It lit our bedrooms, our way home and our trips to the loo after dark. We could see it from miles away, even in the day time, and say, 'That's home.'

There was a funny little antenna - well it looked like one from the ground - which wiggled to and fro when the light was out. Everyone said it stopped wiggling when the light went on, but I don't know how they knew, because it was dark then, and the light went over it, so you couldn't see it. It was switched off when the war began and dismantled not long after when modern technology had made it obsolete.

In many ways we were lucky in our home. It was old and dilapidated. The walls were in such poor condition that Mum had to patch them and cover the patches with brown paper before she could put up wallpaper. We had one cold water tap in the scullery and all hot water was boiled in kettles or in the copper - but we had space. We had four rooms downstairs, which meant that even when we were playing indoors we didn't have to be under Mum's feet - though we often were.

On Sundays we weren't allowed out to play anyway - well only in the backyard which wasn't much fun. Sometimes, on Saturdays, Pop bought each of us a cheap toy, which was duly presented on Sunday - a yo-yo, a jumping frog, a biff-bat, which was a bat with a small ball attached to it by a length of elastic - or some such thing. The novelty usually lasted for the one morning. Indoors on Sunday we were allowed in the Front Room. The fire would be lit in the big duck's nest fireplace, ready for the afternoon and we would be allowed to use the gramophone. My father's music began and ended with military bands so almost all of the records we had were marches - Blaze Away, Old Comrades, Colonel Bogey, Stars and Stripes and so on. We would march round and round the table, changing direction when someone felt like it, and going on till we dropped. Pop thought we showed good taste in music, Mum was almost driven mad. Among the records were a few mavericks, Albert Ketelby's In a Persian Market and In a Monastery Garden and Bells Across the Meadow. I never let on that I actually preferred them to Blaze Away but that is where my love for Classical Music was born and I went in fairly easy stages from Ketelby to Beethoven.

Unlike me, my younger sister, Ella, had a penchant for dolls. At one time, the particular breakfast cereal we used - called, if I remember rightly, Farmers' Glory - gave away little 3 inch high, flat, cut-out wooden figures of people in national costume, each of which slotted into a wooden stand. She collected them all and named them - Ella England - Eric England, Freddie France, Freda France, Nora Norway and so on. She played with them for hours, arranging them in lines and then re-arranging them. It all left me cold, so, while she was thus occupied, I curled up somewhere with a book. I had no time for dolls.

At one point Pop felt really sorry for me because I hadn't got a dolly to play with and he went down to the village shop and bought one for me. Young as I was, I understood why he had done it, but I know he was disappointed in my less than enthusiastic gratitude. I couldn't think what I was supposed to do with it. Later in the day I found the perfect answer. Nellie annoyed me in some way and I whacked her with it. Head, arms and legs flew in different directions and Pop never tried again. I did actually once possess a wax doll. I think I won it or something, but the parents in their wisdom decided not to let me have it to play with and so it was hung over a picture in the front room for me to look at. It never worried me but as a big gesture one day they let me have it to play with - I dropped it and it broke into little pieces. The only doll I did manage to keep for any length of time owed its longevity to the fact that I put it in the bottom of the wardrobe and forgot about it. When it resurfaced, it had little cobwebby cracks all over it, and the rubber that held its legs, arms and head in place had perished. Nellie had a big doll called Joyce but she wouldn't let me touch it. I wonder why?

The grown-ups always made sure that at Christmas time we were well supplied with board games - Ludo, Snakes and Ladders, Chinese Chequers, Mosaics, Draughts, - with any luck, we'd have enough counters left to see us through the winter months. Very early in life, we began to learn all the fun that can be had with a pack of cards - and as soon as we were old enough, we learned to play Whist. Practically every evening, when her work was done, Mum would get out the cards. There were always four people to play Whist and we were taught properly, being thoroughly berated for playing the wrong card. As soon as were considered good enough, we were taken to Whist Drives - two or three every week. I still loving playing Whist. We played Rummy too. Pop lost his temper very easily if he didn't win, and the rest of us ganged up on him. When playing Chinese Chequers, we would watch him carefully building up a long run for himself, and then someone would block up the first hole. He would then sulk and refuse to play. He couldn't abide not winning.

My very earliest memory was of falling out of a doll's pram. I couldn't have been much more than eighteen months old when Nellie decided to put a real doll in her little pram. I can remember being 'parked' by the gate while she nipped up the path to the loo, and, not approving of the situation, I wriggled, the pram tipped up and I fell out. I can clearly recall the sensation of knowing that I was going to fall and yelling. Apart from that, my earliest memories are of the after-dinner time. Nellie would go back to school and Mum would sit at the table reading the paper, so Ella and I had to amuse ourselves. We did this by crawling round and round Mum's feet, which was not very exciting, and the time seemed interminable. I still dislike the hour after lunch more than any other time of day.

Very close to our house was the Methodist Chapel, and so, early in life, we were sent up there to Sunday School. Pop had spent all his youth as a Baptist and only became C of E because Mum was. He wanted us to be Chapel - Mum was only concerned with the convenience. We didn't even have to set foot off the footpath to get to the Chapel. I was still less than five years old, when, at a service, one of the 'big girls' sitting behind me amused herself by digging me in the back. Nellie was at the end of the row and out of reach, so I tried to squirm out of the way. The teacher saw me wriggling, came over and told me to sit still. The next time I wriggled she slapped my legs and shouted at me. My outraged sister promptly took me home and we never went back again. Our flirtation with the Methodists was over.

From then on we went to the Church of England Sunday School, which, at that time, was held in the Day School building. Every Sunday afternoon, we donned our best frocks, hats and shoes and off we went. Only once did we dare to take the short cut home across the field and the result was indelible grass stains on our white canvas shoes. Mum wasn't pleased!

At one point, I am not sure when, they moved the Sunday School into the Church, which was much nearer for us. I think it was probably the coming of a new vicar. We adored him and were terrified of him. We called him 'old Pat.' Unlike the previous vicar, he actually took an interest in the Sunday School and was there every Sunday at 3.45. He was an Irishman with twinkly eyes and a deep chuckle and he told us funny stories - but arrive late or misbehave and you wished you were dead. He took about 10 minutes to open the Sunday School, and then he went home and we all separated into our various classes. On the first Sunday of the month, we had a children's service at 3 p.m. He used to ask us questions during this service which we were expected to answer by singing a verse of a hymn.

'What are you?' he would say, and we would sing,

'We are soldiers of Christ who is mighty to save,
And His banner, the Cross is unfurled.
We are pledged to be faithful and steadfast and brave.
Against Satan, the flesh and the world.'

'What mustn't you do?'

'Do no sinful action,
Speak no angry word.
Ye belong to Jesus,
Children of the Lord.'

There were about eight of these questions and the organist was reduced to a jelly, as she never knew what question was coming and she had to be ready to play whichever tune was needed.

As usual, we had a prize-giving service once a year, prizes being awarded for attendance only - anything over 75% merited a prize. If any child achieved 100%, the vicar figured that the child's mother was worthy of a prize for making sure that the child got there on time every Sunday, so the child had to take his or her mother up to the Chancel steps where she was solemnly presented with a Christmas pudding. Very few were ever won but Ella managed it one year.

Mothering Sunday was special in his time too. The flowers for the mums were all blue violets. Every child had to take his or her mum up to the altar rails to receive the posy.
'You must take her right hand' he said, 'and if there are more than one of you, you must have a finger each.' He did not approve of children coming to the Mothering Sunday Service without their mothers, so no Mum in Church - no posy.

Our annual treats were a party at Christmas and a trip to the seaside in the summer. The catering for the Christmas party was done by the lady who had the Post Office and sweetshop in the village, and always included individual jellies made in ice-cream tubs. We didn't have jelly very often in those days, so everyone jockeyed for places according to which colour jelly they fancied.

We usually played a few games - if anyone was brave enough to organise them - which were followed by a conjurer. We once had the same conjurer doing the same tricks for three years running. By the third year everyone knew what was coming, so the boys who were invited up to help spoilt all the tricks. Before that, one year we had a conjurer who did a bit of ventriloquism as well. He had the usual type of upper class dummy on his knee, and, to our great surprise, this dummy asked for my sister Ella to go up on the stage. Not only did he know her name, but he also knew her nickname, which was only ever used within the family. When the party was over, and we had each received the regulation balloon and orange, we dashed home to tell Mum about this marvellous conjurer - only to find him sitting in the kitchen talking to her. It turned out that he was Auntie Florrie's Uncle Ralph and from then on he became our Uncle Ralph too. He and his wife, Auntie Flo, became great favourites of ours.

The summer trip took us, year after year, to Camber Sands. Two coach loads of excited children would leave the village somewhere about nine o'clock in the morning and we would sing our way to Camber. When we crossed the Rother at Rye, we thought we were nearly there, and the last twisting mile or two seemed unending. In those days, Camber Sands consisted of a very narrow road, lined with bungalows and one or two shops, which led to a small car park and the sand. There was a very small arcade of penny-in-the-slot machines, a helter-skelter and one or two seedy looking cafes and sweet stalls. None of this worried us, we had come for the sea and the sand. The sea was shallow and often a long way out. The sand was never-ending, with huge dunes to the landward side. We couldn't come to any harm there, and we were in and out of the water all day. We spent a lot of time, and very little money, finding and buying presents for the parents. More often than not Mum had a fancy cruet. I hate to think how many she must have had. One I remember was a little yellow car with salt in the bonnet, pepper in the boot and a mustard pot in the middle.

We usually had tea in one of the seedy cafes and then left for home, tired, happy, sunburnt and with sand in our clothes everywhere, clutching our wet swimsuits, the things we had bought and a whole lot of tennis balls that we had dug out of the sand behind the local tennis courts. One year, as an experiment, parents were invited to come with us to relieve the burden on the teachers. They complained that there was nothing to do in Camber - no shops, no amusements - and vowed that they would never let their children go to such a dump again. From then on, we went to Hastings, which had pebbles instead of sand, sea that was deep and rather dangerous for little people and a busy road that ran along beside the beach. We had to cross the main road to get to any shops and there were many distractions that needed money before you could enjoy them. Our 'take-home' presents then were bought in Woolworths together with junky jewellery for ourselves.

When the war came, we couldn't go to the seaside, so we had a summer party in the garden of one of the big houses in the village or in the vicarage garden, with run around games and races. How they managed a tea for us in those days of rationing and shortages I can't think, but there always seemed to be something.

Every year we had a toy service. I can't remember when in the year it was, but we were all expected to take toys that we no longer wanted, to be given to the Baby Castle, a Dr. Barnado home in Hawkhurst. In those days, they didn't expect to be given new toys, as became the habit later on as villagers had more money to spend, but toys that could be mended, painted and put

22

to good use. One year, we took down a whole lot of books, probably most unsuitable, which Pop had tied up with string. Of course the inevitable happened, the string broke and we were frantically trying to tie them all up again with string that was no longer long enough. We went down to the church with armfuls of books that our little arms were quite unable to hold on to for many minutes, so we kept dropping them. Of course we arrived late and we children could have died with embarrassment, though Pop took it all in his stride.

The vicar packed all the toys in his car and took them over to Hawkhurst, and usually took a child or two over with him. One year he took Ella and me, and we were to be at the church at 11 a.m. Of course, we left home with three minutes in which to do a five minute journey, and wondered if he would wait for us. The car was waiting outside the church as we ran round the corner, and he opened the door for us to get in.
'When I say eleven, I don't mean two minutes past.' he growled, and we felt as if we had been beaten. But that was all, reprimand deserved and given, and for the rest of the trip he was his usual jovial self.

When Nellie was confirmed, the service was held in a different parish some seven or eight miles away. Old Pat took our family in his car, and Nellie was furious with me because I was travel sick.
'It isn't a bus,' she stormed at me. 'You have no right to be sick when you are riding in a nice car like that.' I didn't enjoy being travel sick much either.

The vicar was a whiz-kid at maths. When he discovered that I was having difficulties with algebra at school, he gave me private lessons round at the vicarage - an hour at a time once or twice a week. He would give me a string of figures to simplify, full of x's and y's and say,
'I make it 2x. What do you make it?' Fifteen minutes later I'd say,
'I don't make it 2x'
'Don't you? Do it again.' He was never wrong.

He drove an open-topped yellowish-coloured car and would stop and pick up anyone he saw walking.
'Hop in,' he would say, as he held the door open, and then he would take you right home.

At one time, Mum had been ill with 'flu' which had left her very weak. When she thought she was strong enough, she decided to catch a bus to Horsmonden, some two miles away, and walk back. I went with her. She managed to get half-way back and then sat down on a grassy bank, knowing that she could go no further. I didn't know what to do - and nor did she. We saw the vicar go by in his car, the wrong way, and we both wished he was going in the opposite direction. Two minutes later he was back.

'Overdid it, did you?' he said, 'I thought so. Hop in.'

Our old vicar retired just at the time that I was confirmed, and the new one was completely unable to control the boys in Sunday School. They would cheek him, run round the church and generally make his life a misery. He came rather late to the ministry, and didn't foresee the difficulties of having to cope with naughty boys. He had practically no sense of humour, and his one or two attempts at incorporating jokes into his sermons were disastrous. Following a man who told jokes as naturally as breathing, made him feel very inadequate. His voice rose to a high-pitched squeak when he was angry or excited, which the boys used to mimic unmercifully. It was a pity, because he was a very good man and was completely honest in everything. He had no car or any other form of transport, yet he managed to visit all his parishioners on a regular basis going everywhere on foot. When people suggested to him that a car would make life much easier for him, his answer was simply,

'I can't afford one.'

The only two of the Sunday School teachers that I can remember were both as old as God. Olive Baldock lived in a house right in the village, and, as far as we knew, had no life apart from the Sunday School. She rode around on a bicycle with a big basket on the front of it, and when we saw her we would say,

'Hello, Miss Baldock.' in deferential fashion, but we always called her Olive Oil. We made fun of her all the time, but we made sure that she never caught us doing it because we were terrified of her.

Janet Simpson was completely different, gentle, emotional, soft of voice and kind. She lived a mile or so out of the village with her sister, and was a talented artist. In fairly recent years, I have noticed that Janet Simpson's etchings of village scenes have become quite the 'in thing.' I possess one that she gave me herself. She taught the older girls, and at times I was the only girl in her class who attended. I was horrified at the end of that year, to discover that my attendance was given as 87% when I hadn't missed once. She apologised profusely.

'Oh my dear, I am so sorry, but when you were the only one present, I completely forgot to mark the register.' I can't remember whether I ultimately got my prize or not. I expect I did.

She often illustrated her lessons with stories from her own life, and after her sister died, her eyes used to fill with tears whenever she mentioned her. One Sunday, the elastic in her knicker leg broke, and a length of pink locknit began to slide down below her skirt. She was blissfully unaware of it, but we heard very little of what she was trying to teach us that day, as we watched to see how much pink was going to show.

Other teachers came and went. some we liked and some we didn't. None of them could have made much impression on me because I can't remember them. I can remember that every Sunday we sang

> Dear Lord of Thee three things I pray.
> To see Thee more clearly,
> To love Thee more dearly,
> To follow Thee more nearly, day by day.

And I can still remember the tune.

After I was confirmed, they asked me to be a Sunday School teacher, so I was involved with that Sunday School until I was eighteen when I left home to go to college.

When we were considered old enough, we were sent down to the morning service every Sunday as well as attending Sunday School in the afternoon. We sat in a pew just behind the main door, so that we could get out without causing too much of a disturbance, because we were allowed to leave before the sermon started. Nellie would see that we each had a hymn book and a Book of Common Prayer, and she would find the places for us. I thought she was so clever to know where to look for all the different parts of the service, and I was sure that I would never master it. I could read very well and so I followed everything and sang psalms and hymns with great gusto. If we didn't like the hymn before the sermon, we slipped out of church with the first note of the organ, but if it was one of our favourites, we stayed until the very last line before we left.

One thing worried me very much. All the books in the church were inscribed in gold letters.

ALL SAINTS' BRENCHLEY

and I thought that only saints were allowed to use them. I knew that I wasn't a saint, and I was sure that, if any grown-up in the church caught me using them, I would be in serious trouble. I tried to cover up the wording as much as possible, and hoped that no-one would notice. I was inordinately grateful when I was given a Prayer Book of my own for my ninth birthday. I have it beside me as I type. It is very much the worse for wear, but it has been very well used throughout its life.

I joined the choir when I was twelve. Until that time, the choir had been the jealously guarded property of one or two families in the village, but when the war began, the numbers were seriously depleted, and they appealed for more members. My friend and I, both Grammar School girls, joined, together with one dear old lady whose natural speaking voice quavered uncontrollably and her singing was worse. For the first time for years, it was deemed necessary for the choir to have a regular practice night, and a retired headmaster took on the job of choir master. I don't know why the organist didn't do it. The established members of the choir weren't happy at being expected to turn up once a week for practice, as they rather thought that only the recruits needed to be there. They also debated hotly as to whether we newcomers should be allowed to take our place in the choir gallery immediately, or whether it would be advisable to wait until we'd had a certain amount of training. The choir master had the sense to realise that, if we were treated as second class choristers we would soon give up, so choir practice was instituted for everyone, and we all trooped up to the gallery every Sunday morning and evening.

At first, in a desperate attempt to provide four-part harmony, the CM tried to turn me, and the quavery lady, into altos, without much success. She claimed that she found it too hard to sing out of her own register, and I objected to the fact that I could no longer sing my favourite tunes - which is really funny as I became an alto in 1955 and have remained one ever since, deeply resenting any tune I have to sing in unison.

The quavery lady, quite involuntarily, told me one of the funniest things I have ever heard. She was very prim and proper, and one day she was complaining bitterly about the dirty jokes that were told on the forces radio programmes.

'Filthy, they are,' she said, 'really filthy. In fact, on a programme the other day, the jokes were so dirty that even the soldiers in the audience didn't get them!' But she did!!

For one reason and another, the choir fell apart fairly quickly. The turnover of organists was quite rapid and we often had stand-ins. The girl who joined with me soon left and so did the quavery lady. The tenor went off to the war, and sickness hit the older members. The only bass, who was also the verger and the village saddler, was very reliable, but I found quite often that he and I were the only two singers present.

I left the choir when I went away to college and rejoined in 1955. I have been a member ever since.

CHAPTER 4

It was a big day in my life when I went, with Nellie, to school for the first time. She took me into the large infants room and gave me into the care of a plump, motherly person whom I had to call Miss Baker.

'Now, who would you like to sit beside dear,' she asked me. 'Is there anyone here you know.'

I looked fearfully round the room - not a familiar face anywhere. Then I saw a girl I vaguely knew because she lived next door to someone Nellie had once gone to play with, taking me with her.

'I know Joan.' I whispered, much to Joan's surprise. So I was put in a chair next to Joan who proceeded to ignore me.

I can still remember the smell of lead pencils, and the special taste of the minuscule chocolate bars Miss Baker gave as a reward for good work. I was only four years old when I started school and for some time, we little ones were expected to rest for half an hour or so every afternoon. There were beds there so we could lie down properly and possibly go to sleep. The other children did something quiet during this time so as not to disturb us. One very quiet activity I can remember doing during that time when I outgrew the rest period was 'ravelling' or, to be more precise, unravelling. We were each given a metal tray and a small scrap of material, and we had to separate out all the individual threads into the tray. If you were lucky, they came apart easily, but if not, you finished up with a hopeless tangle. I quite enjoyed doing that because I had the patience to fiddle with it and get the threads out properly, and I loved the shimmer of the colours in the tray, but I can't for the life of me understand the educational value of it. The practical value was easier to understand. The older girls made soft toys in their needlework lessons, and we were providing the stuffing.

It was in Miss Baker's class that I learnt to read. I didn't find it particularly difficult, and I easily related reading to spelling and had very little difficulty with that either. I remember when, for the first time, I came across the combination of the two letters 'ur' and I didn't know what they said. Miss Baker wrote 'er' on a piece of paper and asked me what those two letters said. I knew that and I told her. Then she wrote 'ir' and I knew that too. Then you wrote 'ur' and repeated the question. I was puzzled. That was what I had asked her and the deviation into 'er' and 'ir' didn't make much sense to me.

'You stupid child,' she said. 'Ur says er too, just like er and ir.' It still didn't make much sense. After all, if er said 'er' and ir said 'er' why did anyone need something else to say 'er' as well.

I very soon found the joy of 'composition.' Everyone else in the class seemed to hate it but not me. I wrote pages and pages in the most appalling handwriting imaginable. How my teachers managed to plough through it beats me, but the content was good and the spelling was reasonable, so I was always given good marks.

In the playground I played with four boys, one called Frankie and the others all called Roy. We usually played in the sand-pit in the corner of the playground. They all ran around the playground, and I stayed in the sand-pit preparing their dinner for when then they came back. Sexism hadn't been invented then!

One day, in the playground, I was knocked flying by some big girls who were playing chasing, and I had to spend two weeks without going out to play, sporting, round my head, a businesslike bandage which held a pad over a gash just above my eye. I still have the scar. I was so bored I could have screamed. When the two weeks were over, I thought I had better ask if I could go out, so I approached my teacher in the correct fashion, with my hand up, and was completely ignored. I waited very patiently, till someone condescended to notice me and very snappily asked what I wanted.
'Please may I go out to play?' I said. I felt rather like Oliver Twist.
'Of course you can you silly child,' she said. 'Why shouldn't you?'

One thing I learned in the infants class was that the lavatories had to be called 'the offices.' I was used to saying 'the lav,' but no, if nature could not be ignored, I had to raise my hand and ask to go to the offices. These were at the bottom of the playground, behind a fairly high wall and were quite unpleasant. We weren't supposed to play near them, but sometimes the expediency of hiding behind the wall overcame the nastiness of the smell.

It was when I was in the next class, Miss Callow's, that I made the most momentous decision of my life. I was a very amenable kind of child, having discovered, very early in my life, that it was easier to do as one was told than to think up excuses for not doing it. I worked hard and I had a good brain and a good memory. In fact I was a teacher's delight. There were plenty of nuisances in the class who caused mayhem whenever possible, and I really can understand how she felt, during a particularly trying arithmetic lesson, when I dropped my box of counters. It made the most awful clatter as it fell, and counters went everywhere. The worst thing about the whole business was that it was me. She slapped me soundly on my hands and legs and told me to stay in at playtime. I sat and sobbed for twenty minutes while she went off to have her cup of coffee. When she came back - nerves restored, she obviously felt ashamed of the harsh way she had treated me. She picked me up in her arms, smoothed my hair and dried my face, saying,

'Oh come on. It wasn't as bad as all that.' But it was. It was treachery of the worst kind, and completely destroyed my faith in the infallibility of the teaching profession. Little did she know that I was perched up there thinking,

'When I grow up I'm going to be a teacher and then I'll be able to hit children when I feel like it.'

I had very little idea of times. I went to school when Nellie dragged me there, and I went home when someone in authority said it was time to go home, but for all that I quite enjoyed it. As I have said, I liked writing stories and I learned spelling very easily. We used to have spelling bees and I always won. I had no difficulty with 'sums' either, as I liked juggling with figures. I enjoyed acting, and at six years old I knew I did it well. I couldn't draw very well and painting was a disaster, but that didn't worry me. I hated sewing and could spend a whole lesson on the floor looking for a deliberately lost needle.

We seldom had any physical activity at school, but the day came when the Headmistress, Miss Trill, in her wisdom, decreed that, not only would we be having regular PE, from now on, but we would all be dressed alike for it. While making this epic pronouncement she had, on the table in front of her, a pile of mottled grey wool and a pile of navy blue material,

'You will each make yourself a skirt in your needlework lessons, and knit yourself a jumper,' she announced. 'Then your PE uniform will be your navy blue skirt, your grey jumper and long black stockings.'

I was filled with terror. I was only nine and I couldn't knit a row of ten stitches without making an unholy mess of it, and as for sewing a skirt! We were issued with wool, needles and a pattern which I couldn't make head or tail of. Somebody helped me to cast on the correct number of stitches, and I was told to do twenty rows in 'knit one, purl one.' I didn't know how to purl. That knitting stayed in my desk for months, only coming out when it had to. It was a matted, tangled mess. Other girls proudly presented their finished jumpers, mostly done by their Mums, which were held up for the rest of us to see to spur us on. I hadn't even finished the ribbing. I had my place changed and I had to take all my things out of my old desk and put them in the new one, so I carefully left my knitting behind - but it caught up with me. I kept trying to lose it and at last I managed it. I put it in an empty desk, and it was ages before anyone found it. I kept very quiet when the teacher said

'Whose knitting is this?' and no-one remembered it was mine.

'Oh well.' she said, 'It's an utter mess anyway.' and the knitting was pulled off the needles, thrown into the bin and that was the end of that. She never did get her PE classes looking the way she wanted them to, which was just as well really, for a more unhealthy outfit is hard to imagine.

I was about seven when I discovered how easy it is to write poetry. Our teacher was away, and we had to take our chairs and go into the 'big girls room.' The teacher, faced with a massive class to keep occupied, put a selection of 'first lines' on the board, talked a bit about the meaning of rhyme and rhythm and left us all to write poems. In due course, she decided we'd had long enough, and asked various girls to read out their efforts, fulsomely praising any one with the faintest hint of a rhyme or the vaguest suggestion of a rhythm.

'Let's hear something from one of the little ones.' she said, rather condescendingly, and after a while turned to me.

'Read us what you have written, dear.' she commanded. In correct fashion I stood up, cleared my throat and read my poem.

> Through the woods they all came tripping
> Fairies very gay,
> Each one dressed in colours pretty,
> Almost bright as day.

There were three verses but I can't remember any more, which is probably just as well! To use a modern and rather common expression she was gob-smacked.

'The second and fourth lines are a beat short,' she said. 'But it doesn't matter, it doesn't matter at all.' From a distance of sixty-odd years, I can't help wondering why I chose to say 'colours pretty' instead of 'pretty colours.'

Another time our teacher was away, I didn't fare so well. We were told to get on with our sums, which suited me fine. I knew exactly what I was doing and needed no help. I finished the page and turned over, only to be faced with sums I had never seen before, and didn't know how to tackle. They looked like this:-

$$2 \,)\, \underline{\;64\;}$$

I was much too nervous to go and confess to a strange teacher that I didn't know what these sums meant, so I added them all up, and got them all wrong.

It never occurred to me that I was one of the bright pupils. I knew that I was a year younger than most of the girls in my class, but I felt that they looked down on me for that. I 'won the scholarship' to The County School when I was ten, and I still didn't realise that it was anything special.

Our journey home from school - when Mum wasn't working - took us past many challenges. We could, if we liked, climb over a stile into a field and walk to the top of the hill, meeting nothing more dangerous than a cow-pat. We could walk up the road, Blind Lane, and look for violets, wild strawberries or whatever, but mostly we climbed up the bank and walked along the top of it by the fence. This was not easy. There were thorn bushes and holly bushes that grew close by the fence and went right through it. To get between the bushes and the fence meant scratched hands, legs and faces. There were slipways down to the road, but slip was the operative word, and they were generally more dangerous than the prickles.

At the top of the lane was a strangely shaped beech tree - or two. There were two main trunks with a connecting cross-branch rather like a low-level capital H. We spent ages there. A little further on was a wide grass verge culminating in a fairly low bank. Out of this bank grew a sturdy evergreen, with one low branch that grew out over the grass verge. We could climb along that branch very easily, and drop into a pile of leaves. I say 'we' but I always lost my nerve before the drop, and those following me along the branch had to retreat to let me get off. Nellie was furious with me every time, but she still allowed me to have my turn. I never managed it. A little further on was a ditch - a fairly wide one - and beyond it the stump of a long-felled tree. It must have been a big tree judging by the size of that stump. We climbed on to that and jumped the ditch. Opposite that were the chestnut trees which kept us very busy in the late autumn.

Further up, on the other side of the road, was the gap in the hedge where we could climb the spile fence to take the short cut home, but mostly we went by the road to stay with our friends as long as possible.

In the spring, the banks that bordered the lane were a riot of periwinkles, scentless but pretty dog violets, the occasional primrose and white or blue scented violets. Later on there was yellow toadflax - snapdragons - and masses of wild strawberries. We knew where everything grew. There were nests, too, in the hedges, but we knew we mustn't touch - only look. Whenever we found one, we tried to keep it hidden, but the tracks of our feet up the bank always gave it away.

It was on our way home from school that one of the local bullies, who regularly made our lives a misery, amused himself by throwing a wooden coconut-shy ball at us. He missed every time, which was just as well, but we decided we had had enough. There were three of us, Ella, a friend and I, and we could run like hares. We chased him till we caught him, whereupon he threw himself face down onto a bank and covered his head with his arms. We thumped him till our arms ached, and we could see that he was crying. He never touched us again.

When I started school, I drove Nellie mad by my complete inability to hurry. Moaning and grumbling, she would drag me along behind her, and the day when I found, when we were well on our way, that I still had my slippers on, I thought she was going to explode. Still, she fought my battles for me, and when a certain young bully-boy gave me a sharp dig in the ribs as he passed, and knocked me over, she was after him like an angry dog. She caught him and boxed his ears soundly before coming to see if I was hurt. When it was my turn to be the big sister, I found that Ella's will was stronger than mine. At that time, we took sandwiches to school in an attache case, and Mum decreed that I should carry the case in the morning, when it was full, and Ella should carry it home in the afternoon, when it was empty, - only she wouldn't, and I had to carry it both ways. To make the point clear, she put it down in the road at the bottom of the hill, and I was the one who cracked first and went back for it.

Later on, we had school dinners, and one day she refused to eat her pudding. She had asked for a small one and had been given a large one, so she sat and looked at right through dinner play. The headmistress saw that this was a battle that she wasn't going to win, so in an attempt at face-saving, she decreed,

'Well, if she won't eat it, her sister must.' Have you ever known anything so unfair?

I will never forget my first taste of school custard - it was horrible. I couldn't understand what they'd done to it. I loved custard at home but there was no similarity at all - even the colour was different. It wasn't until I was grown-up that I discovered what was wrong - they used lemon-flavoured custard. I like things that are lemon-flavoured, the stronger the better, but not that custard.

School dinners were cooked in the canteen, a glorified shed at the back of the school, and served in the ordinary classrooms. Ten minutes before the end of the morning, we had to clear our desks, which were pushed together in long rows and then we were given American cloth table covers and two spoons and a fork for each place. We weren't given knives, as nothing we had to eat ever needed cutting. All the meat was minced - minced meat pie, minced meat roly-poly pudding, mince on its own, shepherd's pie, potato cheese, I can't remember anything else - so we ate our first course with a spoon and fork and our sweet - with or without custard - with a spoon only. I seem to remember lots of ground rice with jam, boiled rice, tapioca, semolina, all of which I hated, prunes and custard, rhubarb and custard - I really didn't do very well on the puds. We had senior girls as servers who were supposed to ask you what you wanted and get it for you. If they liked you it was fine, but if they didn't, you had what you were given and you were made to eat every scrap of it. All the food came in flat trays or huge white enamel bowls, and the teachers dished it out, using huge ladles. We begged Mum to let us have sandwiches again and in the end she did.

The boys and girls attended different schools in the same building. There was a headmaster and a headmistress who each took the top class. The school was approached by a path which led straight up to the centre of the verandah. There was one classroom with a door situated centrally on the verandah, and one either end - girls to the left, boys to the right. In warm weather the classroom doors would be open, but the children were not

expected to look along the verandah at their opposite number. Frequently the Headmaster would appear in the girl's room, point an accusing finger at someone, and announce dramatically - everything he did was dramatic - 'That girl was looking at my boys.' The usual punishment was:-
'If you want to look at them, go and join them.' which was sheer hell for some and sheer heaven for others.

In 1935 we celebrated the Silver Jubilee of King George the Fifth and Queen Mary, and two years later the Coronation of King George the Sixth and Queen Elizabeth. For both of these occasions we had to learn some Country Dances - Rufty Tufty was one of them and Hunsdon House was another. I vaguely remember learning Gathering Peascods too, and it must have been for one of those occasions because we never did dancing at any other time - there wasn't any space big enough to do it on a regular basis.

The girls who were dancing as girls wore pretty floral dresses that came down to their ankles, and the ones dancing as boys wore country smocks and red neckerchiefs. I was a boy and so I didn't get to wear one of those pretty frocks. I have done much Country Dancing since those days and I have almost always danced as a boy. Maybe infant school days have more influence than we realise.

Both of these celebrations were planned to take place in the garden of one of the huge houses in the village, and one of them did. For the other one it rained, and the whole affair was transferred to the village hall which wasn't really big enough. I can't remember which was which.

Every year we did a concert. Each class produced some sort of a play or entertainment and the older children did 'the big play.' When I was in the infants, for two years running we had to do the same play about the rainbow. I can't think why. There were seven rainbow fairies dressed in crepe paper skirts and wings. My favourite colour was (and is) red, but could I be the red fairy - not likely! The first time I was orange and the second time I was green. I can remember holding out an orange and announcing,
'O is for orange. This is an orange. I am the Orange Fairy.'
Gripping stuff!

One year when I was in the Junior School, the 'big play' was The Water Babies and I was a water baby. Mum said it was the best bit of type-casting she'd ever known. I didn't have anything to say, which didn't suit me one bit, but I quickly learnt all the words that any water baby had to say and if anyone was away I stood in for them. I finished up with more to say than any of them. We had to wear white vests and skirts of crepe paper strips that were supposed to look like seaweed. When the local newspaper sent a photographer, they discovered that my costume had been overlooked and I hadn't got one. They wouldn't even let me stand at the back without a proper costume, so I wasn't in the picture. There's no justice in this world! They imported two sisters who had already left the school to be Mrs. Do-as-you-would-be-done-by and Mrs Be-done-by-as-you did, which I thought was a bit naughty.

Somewhere around Christmas time every year, there was a party, always known as Payne's Party, given for all the schoolchildren except the infants, in the Village Hall. It was very similar to the Sunday School party except that there were many more children there. The war put a stop to that. The infants had a party of their own, and I can remember a Christmas tree with identically dressed little dollies sitting around the trunk. The big girls had dressed them, and each one had a knitted dress, cape, knickers and bonnet and they really looked lovely. They were all done in different colours, but did I get a red one - I did not.

Just once there was a trip to Hastings for everyone in the girl's school except the infants. Although Hastings was less than thirty miles away, there were many children in the school who had never seen the sea, and I think the trip was to remedy that. Whether it proved to be too much hassle or too expensive or what I don't know but it was never repeated. Of course the war put an end to anything of that nature anyway.

As might be expected, we three sisters went through most of the childish ailments, singly or together. In those days quarantine was a very serious business, and strictly adhered to, and as we had measles, one after the other, not one of us could go to school while a single spot existed. One way and another we had about six weeks at home, and when the Attendance Officer came round to see why Mum was keeping us at home, he received very short shrift.

'Do you think I actually want the three of them under my feet all day?' she asked him. 'Two of them are perfectly well and I'd love to send them to school. Are you going to give me permission to do so?' He retreated in haste.

I had chicken pox all to myself, except that I generously passed it on to Uncle Frank. Being an adult, it made him very ill, and I can still picture him sitting on the little chair in front of the fire with his head in his hands, moaning in pain. Our doctor called in another doctor to give a second opinion, as he began to fear that Uncle had really contracted smallpox. He hadn't though. I caught whooping cough in my pre-school years. Mum said that she had to admire my tenacity. I was always a chatter-box, and I would be in the middle of a sentence when a fit of coughing caught me and, as she said, I would cough my heart up and then carry on with what I was saying as though I'd not been interrupted. German measles came in my second year at the Grammar School and again I had it to myself. I never had mumps. Ella and Eric succumbed at different times, and though I have taught through several mumps epidemics, the germs have left me severely alone. Right at the end of her school career, Ella developed almost all the symptoms of scarlet fever and, to be on the safe side, the doctor had her admitted to the isolation hospital. Once there she had to stay for the normal length of time, whether she actually had the disease or not. She always maintained that she didn't. After she had been taken away, a man came in to fumigate the room where she had been sleeping. He sealed up the window, the door and any obvious cracks in the floorboards, and then lit a special kind of candle thing and told us not to go in until the next day. As I had been sleeping in the room with her for years, the whole operation seemed a trifle superfluous, so we unsealed it at bedtime and I slept in there as usual with no ill-effects.

I was rather worried one day when Miss Trill announced that she wished to see two girls at playtime - and I was one of them. I racked my brains to think of what I might have done wrong but to no avail. When the time came, she told us that we were the only two girls in the school not sporting the navy-blue beret that she wanted everyone to wear. There was no such thing as a school uniform in those days, at least, not for an ordinary village school and, as might be expected, I wore a bright red beret. The other sinner wore a green one.

'Tell your Mummies to buy you a navy-blue beret as soon as possible.' we were told.

'WHAT!' said Mum when I reported back to her. 'I spend my money as I see fit and I will buy my children what I like. I'm going down to see that woman.' I never knew when she went or what was said but I continued to wear my red beret and not another word was said. Miss Trill never liked my mother, and it must have been very galling to her to know that Mum's daughter was one of her brightest pupils.

The green-hatted child was a girl named Sheila who was always in and out of trouble. She lived some three miles away from the school and had to travel on the service bus which did a special mini-run for the school children a few minutes after school closed, and then there wasn't another one until after 5 pm. One afternoon, Miss Trill kept Sheila after school to do her sums again, and made her miss the bus home. Imagine the outcry if that happened now! When she had finished, Miss Trill put a line straight through them and told her to do them again. Sheila returned to her place and sat down, then quite deliberately, she picked up all the things on her desk, one by one, and threw them at Miss Trill - pen, pencil, ruler, rubber, sum book, exercise book and finally the heavy wooden inkstand. Then she walked home.

Miss Trill's influence on my family was longer lasting than she deserved, but not for good. As I said she did not like Mum. Mum believed in straight speaking, and would kow-tow to nobody when it came to things that she considered to be hers by right. All of Mum's children were bright enough to have passed the scholarship for the Grammar School, but I was the only one who got there. When Nellie was of the right age, her teacher said to Mum,
'She's a very bright little girl. Wouldn't you have liked her to try for a scholarship?' Mum said,
'Of course I want her to. What do I have to do?'
'Oh I think it's too late. Names had to be in two or three weeks ago.'
'Well, why didn't anyone tell me? How was I supposed to know?' The teacher said she would do what she could, but it was indeed too late, and Nellie never had her chance. Miss Trill's dislike of Mum had overridden her duty to do the best for her pupils.

Five years later it was my turn. My father, who adored Nellie and had little time for me, was still smarting over the way she was overlooked and he said, quite firmly, that if one daughter didn't have a chance then the second one shouldn't have it either. Mum took the view that depriving both daughters wouldn't help anyone, and insisted that I should sit for The

Scholarship and, as usual, Mum prevailed. I didn't know any of this till years later. All I knew was that I was taken to the Grammar School to take an examination and in due course I went to that school. When it was Ella's turn, two years later, she stated quite categorically that she had no intention of taking the exam as she didn't want to go to another school. Whether it was fear of competition, fear of failure or first-hand knowledge of all the homework I had to do, I don't know, but she remained at the village school until she was 14.

Five years later, when Eric was eleven the whole education system was in a state of flux. The new secondary school a few miles away was in use, and the older children from the village schools were being moved down in stages. Somehow, Eric lost his chance, but he did go to the Technical School for the last two years of his education. so, as it turned out, I was the only one to get a Grammar School education, which wasn't at all fair. I don't say I shouldn't have had it, but the others should have had a fair crack of the whip too. They did benefit from my scholarship though, as grants in those days were reasonably generous and, thanks to friends who handed down outgrown school uniform to me, Mum had to spend very little on my school clothes. My bus season ticket was provided - and I could use it whenever I liked, two or three times a day if I wanted to and any time during the weekend - my school dinners were paid for and Mum managed to keep all of us clothed on the grant money she got for me.

CHAPTER 5

My life changed abruptly when I transferred to the County School. To start with, I had to leave home at 8 o'clock in the morning and I didn't get home again until about 5.15. As soon as I had finished my tea, I was banished into the front room to do my homework. At first I had an hour's homework, but in the second year it was increased to an hour and twenty minutes, and it kept increasing. As a result, I was no longer able to get out to play with the other children and was regarded as stuck-up and big-headed because of it. I wasn't stuck-up or big-headed, just terribly lonely. Not only that but, unlike all the other children, I had to wear a school uniform, navy blue coat or blazer, navy blue gym-slip, white blouse, dusky grey long socks or stockings and brown shoes. In the summer we were allowed to wear dresses in pink, blue, green or old gold gingham, white socks and sandals. The dresses had to be made up in the standard pattern, straight bodice, full skirt and short puff sleeves for the Junior School, and a shirt-waisted pattern with a box-pleated skirt and straight short sleeves with a white cuff for the Senior School. These clothes were very expensive, even though most of mine were passed to me by an older girl, and so I had to wear them for best as well as for school, which meant six days a week of uniform.

On my first day at my new school, I donned my new uniform and went down to the village to catch the 8.10 bus. An older girl was to keep an eye open for me, but she boarded the bus later on. Having arrived at school, all the new pupils were collected together in the hall, form lists were read out and then we followed an older girl to our new formroom. We had had no previous visits to get to know the school, and no introductory schemes of any kind, which made it all very strange and frightening. To make matters worse, I had always suffered from travel sickness - I still do (don't anyone try to tell me that it is purely psychological) - and twice in the first week I spent the morning in the sick-room, much to the annoyance of the gym mistress, who read me a lecture as long as your arm.

After a bewildering morning of getting used to a different teacher for every subject, we were once more congregated in the hall in order to learn the routine for school dinner. This was served in the gymnasium, and we had to lead up from the hall, pick up a chair on the way and fill up the tables in rotation. Each table seated eight girls including one table prefect who had to serve out the food. Never was anyone more careful to see that a plate pie was cut exactly into eight equal pieces, each with a 45 degree angle that could have been measured with a protractor.

I walked up the hill from the village that evening with my head in a complete whirl, wondering how long I could put up with it all. As soon as I got indoors, I had to change out of my uniform and put on play clothes - although I didn't have time to play. Then it was tea, homework and a little free time before I went to bed. One evening, I felt so frustrated that I flicked my pen above my head and left a trail of ink spots right across the ceiling. It was weeks before anyone noticed it, and then, one Sunday at tea time, Pop was swinging back in his chair and as he looked up he saw it. The most infuriating thing about it was that we got slapped for swinging our chairs the way he was doing. I never got punished for those ink spots, I don't know why.

I had exactly one year at the County School and then war broke out and the whole world changed. The hard tennis courts-cum-netball pitches had huge zig-zagged trenches dug across them, which were reinforced and roofed over to make air-raid shelters with sufficient room for everyone in the school. The entrances were in the bank. While these were being constructed, the windows of the cloakrooms were bricked in to provide a limited amount of shelter, and we all went to school for three half days a week. As more shelter became available, the three half days became four, then five until finally we got back to full time schooling.

At home we quickly got used to rationing. We all gave up having sugar in our tea so that mum could make jam. At first we had saccharin instead, but it left a bitter taste so we gave up sweetening altogether. Living in the country as we did, we had vegetables from our own garden, eggs from our own hens and a rabbit when anybody caught one. Mum became expert at making a little go a long way, and we never went hungry, but we learned not to be fussy about food. A valuable lesson, that.

When the serious bombing started, we would lie in bed at night and hear the interminable throb-throb of the German planes, as wave after wave of them passed overhead on their way to London. I was rigid with fear and completely unable to get to sleep, but Ella slept soundly. Mind you, the positions were reversed when there was a thunder-storm. Then she lay rigid with fear and I went to sleep. I had more trust in God than in the Germans. We could hear the CRUMP of anti-aircraft fire, and we knew that a hit German bomber would jettison its bombs and run for home, and that was when we could be hit. When the all-clear sounded in the early hours, we grabbed what sleep we could because it was school as usual in the morning.

We had to carry our gas masks with us wherever we went. When they were issued to us, they were in flimsy cardboard boxes rather like Easter egg boxes with a lid over the top. We all bought plastic covers for the boxes, with long straps so that we could carry the things over our shoulder and leave our hands free. Then gas mask shaped holders appeared on the market, which were far less cumbersome but not so protective for the gas mask, and we all had those. We regarded the whole business as a complete nuisance, but we didn't dare leave the things at home. We also had to carry identity cards which most of us tucked into the top of our gas mask cases.

Because of our proximity to the coast, our village was in a restricted area, just. The demarcation line was just outside Tunbridge Wells. We had no idea what this meant until one day Ella and I went into the town to go to the pictures. That was a disastrous trip altogether as we were supposed to be met off the bus by Auntie Florrie, only she wasn't there. Completely lost by this, we walked round to the cinema to see if she was waiting there. She wasn't. We waited around for nearly an hour, and, as she didn't turn up, we caught the next bus home. Just outside the town the bus was stopped at a check point, just like all the best war films, and ARP officials came through the bus looking at everybody's papers. We hadn't got any papers and they bullied us unmercifully. At one point we thought that they weren't going to let us go home, and we were practically in tears. What danger they imagined a couple of small girls could be I don't know. Anyhow, in the end they let us go on, they wouldn't have known what to do with us otherwise. That was the only time we were ever stopped there in the whole of the war. Just to tidy off the story, Auntie Florrie had gone in to the cinema without us. Apparently our bus was a bit late and she had another child with her. She decided that they would miss the beginning of the film if she waited for us, and that was that.

The day that war was declared, Ella and I happened to be staying with Auntie Florrie and Uncle Frank just outside Ramsgate. As Uncle had been a regular soldier, he was on the reserve list. On the previous day, the radio had announced that all reserve soldiers were not to wait for their calling up papers, but were to report to their depots without delay. He had left on the next train, leaving his wife in a complete flap, not knowing what to do about us, or indeed herself. She had sent a message home to Mum to come and get us immediately, and had then decided to move in with a friend in similar circumstances some three miles away, so that whoever came to get us would have been unable to find us. I explained this angle of the situation to her but she said she couldn't help that. In any event, we were still at her home when Pop arrived for us. The first air-raid siren went off that morning and we all dashed down into the Anderson shelter. Auntie took rather a long time to come down and when she did she was wearing her gas mask.

In 1940 we had a bomb disposal squad stationed in the village. A very harassed officer came round and asked Mum if she had room for one or two of the soldiers, and when she hesitated he explained that she would of course be issued with quite generous extra rations as well as being paid a very reasonable lodging fee. He also stressed that if he was unable to find enough people who would take them voluntarily, he would have to start again on a compulsory basis. So Johnny and Charlie joined the family.

Charlie was a large, slow moving, inarticulate son of Birmingham who wrote long letters to his wife two or three times a week. Johnny was a little Yorkshireman who never stopped talking but found writing to his wife a near impossibility. Charlie made very little impression on us. He was kind, withdrawn, quiet and always correct but basically he was just there. Johnny was different. As he jumped down from the army lorry that delivered them to us, he called out to Mum,
'Can you make a Yorkshire pudden, Ma? If not, I'll teach you.'
'Cheeky monkey.' said Mum.

He always called her 'Ma' which none of us would have dared to do. He teased us and played with us, and although we had difficulty at first understanding his Yorkshire accent we adored him. Being small and nippy, it was his job, when an unexploded bomb was located, to go down into the crater and see what was what. Depending on what he found, the bomb was either defused or detonated safely. Sometimes when he got down into the crater he heard the bomb ticking, which meant that it was still alive and liable to go off. That was when he needed to move quickly. Once or twice after such an experience he was quite ill next day. He called it 'a poorly do.' We would now call it stress, shock or trauma. He had, quite illegally, a fin from a German bomb which he intended to take home as a keepsake. Whenever he had a 'poorly do,' Mum had to hide the fin in case the army doctor saw it when he came to look him over to check that he wasn't skiving.

The people in the village who knew them were very sad when our 'bomb boys' were posted. They had caused no trouble and had been very much a part of the village. We recognised them for what they were - family men, heartsick at being separated from their loved ones. Charlie wrote Mum a very correct letter, thanking her for her kindness to him and signing it 'from your best lodger' and that was the last we ever heard of him. As they climbed into the lorry that took them away, Johnny called out,
'I'll be back, Ma. I'll come back and see you.' and he did too, once or twice, until he was posted overseas. He kept in touch with us right through the war, and I had letters from North Africa and Italy. I forget what they called those letters. You had a special form to write on, and you could only write on one side. The letter was then photographed in miniature and sent over to be returned to its correct size before being delivered. Normal letters were censored and took much longer to arrive. These were more fun though, because he would write the maddest things - steamy Hollywood-style love letters, letters written in huge block letters, 'in case you aren't hearing too well' and occasionally a blank page 'this is for anyone who can't read.'
Although the letters were mostly addressed to me, we all read them and laughed and cried over them, and recognised them as a form of release from the horrors he was living through. We lost touch with him after the war until, a year before he died in 1991, he tried to trace us by writing to the village Post Office. This had changed hands several times since his day, and we girls were all married and no longer in the village. But, as luck would have it, the postmaster showed the letter to my cousin who passed it on to me.

During the Battle of Britain, the bombers that were on their way to London passed right over our heads. There were anti-aircraft guns and searchlights all round us, and Spitfires and Hurricanes were busy in the hours of daylight. From the top of the hill, we could look towards London and see the barrage balloons that were the next line of defence. We became quite used to throwing ourselves flat on the floor, wherever we were, when we heard the whine of falling bombs, preferably under a roof of some kind, however flimsy, but very often in the open air. Pop cracked his head against the bread crock as he went down in the pantry one day and that was our one and only war wound.

For a short time, while the Battle of Britain was at its height, we all slept downstairs under various tables, but it was too cramped and uncomfortable to put up with for long, so we took our chances in our own beds. During the day we were in the fields, where Mum was picking plums or apples, and so were able to watch the dog fights going on over our heads. We saw hundreds of planes in the sky, heard bursts of machine gun fire and saw plumes of black smoke billow out from a stricken plane. We cheered if it was an enemy plane and groaned if it was one of ours. One day, a falling German bomber suddenly changed direction and veered straight towards the orchard where we were working. The foreman panicked and hustled us first one way and then another until we finally took matters into our own hands and crouched under a tall hedge that bordered the orchard. The bomber hit the top of the hedge as it went over, showering us with twigs and leaves. It appeared to crash in the next field, but appearances are deceptive and it actually landed about three miles away as the crow flies.

On another occasion, Ella and I were picking damsons in a private garden at the other end of the farm. Damsons were not particularly easy to get hold of, but one of Mum's workmates had a tree of them in her garden and, knowing Mum's weakness for damson jam, let her have all she wanted - as long as she arranged to get them picked. We perched ourselves high up in the tree, which was on high ground anyway, and picked damsons in a desultory fashion as we watched the air battle raging above us. When we returned to Mum she was almost frantic with worry.
'Why didn't you come back when the siren sounded?' she demanded. Quite honestly, the idea never occurred to us.

We would count the parachutes as they descended, white ones were 'ours' and black ones were 'theirs' - or vice versa, I can't really remember. At times the sky seemed to be full of them, there was no need to exaggerate the numbers. The story goes that one local fellow, sitting on the Jubilee Seat, which had a commanding view over the valley, suddenly found that a dead German airman had landed at his feet. He joined two other Germans in the Churchyard with plain wooden crosses marking their graves. The War Graves Commission paid my Dad a regular wage to keep the graves tidy - he was the Churchyard gardener at the time. Some people complained bitterly at having the enemy buried in our churchyard, but most people said , 'They're all some mothers' sons.' After the war the bodies were removed for reburial elsewhere.

When the flying bombs started, we were in a whole new ball game. No longer could the sirens warn us of danger, the wretched things just kept coming. We would hear the high-pitched whine of the engine and stand still and listen for it to stop. If it carried on over us, we breathed a sigh of relief, but if the engine stopped, we dived for cover because that meant it was coming down. We soon learned the flight paths that they followed, one came straight over our house and another one went along behind the trees at the other side of Mr. Prior's (one-time Mr Lawrence's) field.

One morning, I came out of the loo at the end of the garden and saw one coming straight towards me, not making a sound. Its nose was pointing earthwards, and I didn't see how it could possibly miss our house. I was too petrified to move. At what seemed like the last moment, it tipped sideways. Being on the top of a hill saved us as well for it fell in our primrose woods at the bottom of the hill. We lost our bedroom ceilings with that one. Mum was still in bed and the plaster came down all over her. The local builder came round to assess the damage, and after taking a good look, he said,
'I'm going to pretend I haven't been here yet. I'll come back this afternoon. While I've gone, you youngsters get to work and pull down as much of the rest of that plaster as you can. If you do that, you'll get a whole new ceiling out of the authorities. As it is now, it'll just be patched.' We had a lovely time and we got new ceilings.

One evening, during the Battle of Britain, there was a knock at the door and, as usual, Pop went to answer it. When he came back in, he had a soldier with him. We never did find out why he knocked on our door that night. Apparently when Pop opened the door the conversation went as follows :-
'Yes?'

'It's only a corporal.'

'Well you'd better come in.' - Pop would have invited the devil himself in if he'd been wearing khaki - and so Corporal Jack Jones from somewhere in Wales joined the family. We children were still reeling from the loss of Johnny and Charlie and were delighted to have another soldier around. He used to turn up at any time and we treated him like a big brother. He enjoyed playing whist and came to all the whist drives with us. There was an ammunition dump in some woods about two miles away and that's where he was stationed. One day, there was a fire on a nearby farm where there were horses, and somehow he got involved in the rescue work. One of the horses was trapped and screamed in terror before it died. He came up to us when it was all over, looking absolutely ghastly, and all he could say was 'That poor horse,' which he repeated over and over again all evening.

After a while his visits became less frequent, and he came to the whist drives squiring a rather charmless lady who lived alone because her husband was away at the war. We were puzzled and hurt but, looking back, I realise that I alone held the key to why this happened. I was at home alone with Mum one afternoon when he dropped in. As usual Mum made a cup of tea and we sat and chatted. After a while, I needed to go to the loo, so I went out of the back door and up to the end of the garden. When I came back the back door was locked. I thought that he was playing a trick on me, and I wasn't going to give him the satisfaction of hearing me yell to be let in, so I waited a while, but as nothing happened, I went round to the pantry door, which was not locked, and went in. I found Mum on her back on the floor with Jack kneeling over her, pinning her arms down. Of course he got up in a hurry when I walked in and, while I was helping Mum to her feet, he quickly left the house. I was a complete innocent, and still feeling rather ill-used at being locked out, so when Mum said to me, 'Don't tell anyone about this.' I rather wondered why she thought I'd want to, and I promptly forgot all about it. It is only since I began writing this that the incident has come back into my mind. Rape was a word I had never heard and, although I vaguely knew the facts of life, that knowledge had no great importance in my scheme of things. Now, of course, I realise only too well why Corporal Jack Jones from somewhere in Wales ceased to visit us.

One thing the war did for all of us was to teach us the true value of things. We learned to abhor waste in any shape or form. Clothes were worn until they were worn out, and even then we made something else from the good bits. The amount of clothing coupons one was allowed meant that if you bought a new coat, that was it until the next year's coupons were issued. A pair of shoes, a skirt or dress, wool for a jumper or a cardigan and you had none left for anything else. I made blouses out of any bits of material that came to hand, very often using two or more different materials in one garment, and jumpers out of darning wool, with all the little bits of wool tied together and the knots hanging inside. A big bonus was parachute silk - or nylon - which was coupon-free and came in huge panels large enough to make a dress. It was very delicate looking but was as tough as leather and lasted for ever. I made Mum a couple of nightdresses which she wore for years and years. The sewing silk rotted and I had to restitch them completely, twice, but the material was as good as new. She finally got rid of them, long after the war, because she was sick to death of them.

I even made sandals out of clothes line. It was a tough job but they were wearable and comfortable and cheap. You begged, borrowed, stole or, as a last resort bought, a length of clothes line which you twisted into the shape of the sole of a sandal. You also needed some coloured braid - like school PE bands, and some strongish material or an inner sole to line them with. Then it was just a matter of sewing it all into place, which needed a very strong needle and brute force. Still those things were not on ration and we did almost anything to save coupons.

It was amazing how economical one learned to be with things like butter and sugar, when you knew quite well that, once it was used up, there would be no more until the next week's rations arrived - no matter how much money you had. No food of any kind was ever wasted. Leftovers - which were few in any case - were used up in some shape or form next day, however heavily disguised. We also learned to make full use of the wild fruits that were God-given. Throughout the early autumn, we would make regular trips to all the thickets and hedges where wild blackberries grew. We ate them in pies and puddings and just plain stewed. Mum made jam and jelly and put pounds and pounds into kilner jars to preserve them for the winter months. We also collected elderberries for wine. I still make elderberry wine the same way my Mum did and I have never tasted better. She used to put the wine to ferment in huge stone bottles, and, when fermentation was finished, the bottle was corked and left till Christmas, when there was always at least one bottle each of elderberry and rhubarb. Pop was the one who broached the bottles, and the procedure never varied.

He would take a quart milk jug out into the pantry and fill it up. He would then pour himself a glass to check that it was up to standard. If he was doubtful, he would repeat the procedure until he was satisfied. Then he brought the jug into the kitchen and poured out a glassful for every adult present, including himself. After that, we children each had a little in the bottom of a glass, and then he finished up what was left. When the bottles were empty that was that until next Christmas.

Nellie joined the WAAF in 1941 and spent the rest of the war on various Bomber Command bases in and around Lincolnshire. We were very much aware of the dangers of these places being bombed, and looked forward to the times when she came home on leave to the 'safety' of Kent. As she spent most of her leave writing letters to the people she had left behind, and moaning at us for being 'childish,' we very soon left her to her own devices, and breathed a sigh of relief when her leave was over. At one time she and Uncle Frank, an imposing Military Policeman, met up on leave and, as luck would have it, a flying bomb went over. Neither of them had seen one before, and they went quite pale and ran round in small circles while the rest of us, mere civilians, stood and watched it, and calculated reasonably accurately where it was likely to fall.

As the war drew to its close, I was busy in my spare time knitting myself a jumper out of any scraps of wool I could find lying about. The result, a multi-coloured striped garment, was enough to blind the feeble and I was advised to put off wearing it until the war was over. It would, I was told, be a celebration in itself. I was at home alone when the news broke so, when it was time for Mum to come home, I donned my stripes and went down the road to meet her. She knew as soon as she saw me coming that the war was over.

In our innocence, we thought that everything would return to normal almost immediately, but that was not the case. Rationing was continued for a long time after the war ended, and was gradually phased out as supplies became more readily available. Other things changed immediately, like the fact that the blackout was lifted and houses showed lights again. I was particularly glad of this one night, when the last bus home from the town was full, and, at 8 pm. left half a dozen of us standing forlornly at the bus stop with no way of getting home. Two of us, both girls of sixteen, decided to walk and set off on the seven mile trek. We really did appreciate the sight of lighted windows that night.

When my brother first saw the headlights of cars in the distance, he was really frightened. He was only five when war broke out, and had seen very few cars at night, and those had sheets of tissue paper, or something similar, over their lights to dim them.

During my years as a teacher, I have often met the attitude that living through the war must have been fun. Modern children tend to think that dodging bombs and watching dog-fights in the sky was high adventure. My answer has always been the same. I spent the formative years of my life being scared all the time. It taught me a lot, but by and large it wasn't fun.

CHAPTER 6

These days, when I jockey for a place to park the car while I do the weekly shopping, I thing longingly of the way that Mum did hers. When she and Pop first set up home, the local tradesmen were quick off the mark to ask for her custom. Within days she was provided with a grocer, a baker, a butcher and a milkman. In each case she accepted the first one who came and remained a customer all the time she was satisfied with their service. In my young days, the butcher called twice a week, and he knew Mum's requirements almost as well as she did. We always had a joint on Sunday and we ate the remainder cold on Monday with bubble-and-squeak, because it was washing day and she didn't have time to prepare fresh vegetables. We had sausages for breakfast on Sundays, unless she had bought a joint of pork for dinner, in which case we had salmon and rice as she considered that two lots of pork would be too rich for us. On Saturdays we had beef pudding, which Nellie hated. Mum loved to tell the tale of the time, before I was born, when she was wall-papering, and Pop had gone to be fed at his mother's. At midday, Nellie happily ate the boiled egg with bread and butter soldiers followed by an orange that Mum had provided for their dinner, and then remarked,
'Wasn't that a lovely dinner Mummy, and I expect Daddy's only got an old beef pudding!'

Meals were planned to fill us up as cheaply as possible, so puddings featured quite heavily. Bacon pudding was a great favourite - rashers of bacon laid on a rectangle of suet crust and rolled up into a roly-poly pudding. Similarly, a sausage pudding made a regular appearance. We didn't mind, we loved them. Toad-in-the-hole, neck of mutton stew (it wasn't all called lamb in those days!), meat pie, with more pie than meat, these were our dinners. Rabbits were quite often on the menu but they didn't come from the butcher!

We always had a pudding. Throughout the winter, all the fruit that Mum had bottled came out to make puddings and pies or to be stewed and eaten with custard. She reckoned that there should be fresh rhubarb from the garden for a pudding on Easter Sunday, and fresh gooseberries for Whit Sunday. As the kitchen range was almost always alight, it was no trouble to pop things into the oven or put a pudding on to boil or steam, so we had fig pudding, date pudding, orange pudding, lemon pudding, ginger pudding, chocolate pudding and the favourite, Brown George. Someone once said to Pop,

'I understand your wife has a super recipe for chocolate pudding, Will you ask her if she'd write it out for me?'

'No need for that,' said Pop, 'I can tell you how to do it. You just make an ordinary chocolate pudding and put custard over it.'

In the summer, when there was masses of fruit about, she often made a summer pudding. I have, in recent years, seen in several places, recipes for summer pudding, but none of them were like Mum's. She lined a large basin with slices of bread, filled it to the brim with any raw soft fruit that was available, put another slice of bread on the top, and then put a plate on it with a 5lb weight from her kitchen scales to squash the fruit down and release the juices. It was delicious. She never soaked the bread first and wouldn't have dreamed of stewing the fruit as modern recipes say.

The baker called every week on Tuesday, Thursday and Saturday and from him Mum bought bread, and only bread. He carried cakes and 'fancies' but Mum never bought them. Every bit of cake we had was home-made - fruit cake, chocolate cake, coffee cake, lemon, orange, ginger, date, fig, coconut, - never a trace of icing or decoration, never sandwiched together with jam or cream. The only cake that was ever decorated in any way was the Christmas cake and Uncle Frank iced that. Mum made a cake every Saturday which was new for Sunday tea and then it came out every day until it was eaten. We were allowed one slice only, and by the time the cake was almost finished it was very dry. Of course, as the week progressed and the cake grew less and less attractive, most of the family had an extra slice of bread and spurned the cake altogether, so its life was prolonged. I always had my slice of cake, however dry it was, because if Mum felt that it really had gone too far, she let me have jam on it. She made cheese scones during the week - lovely when fresh but hard going when they were two or three days old. She made quite a lot of pastry, as we often had meat or fruit pie for dinner, and with left-over pastry she would make jam tarts. She disliked cooking, it was just something that had to be done, so nothing was ever fancy.

'I'm a good plain cook.' she used to say, and plain was the operative word. The nearest she ever got to embellishment was to put spirals or diamonds on the tops of her pies, and that was merely to use up the bits of pastry.

'You mustn't put too much filling into tarts.' was another of her maxims. There was no danger of jam bubbling over the top of her jam tarts or of mincemeat leaking out of her mince pies. This is one point where I disagree entirely with my mother. I put as much filling into a tart as I can get, but then, I don't have to watch money or rations as she did.

The milkman, of course came every morning. He brought the milk in huge churns, and measured it out in pints into Mum's jugs. Every morning she would leave one or two jugs on the table just inside the pantry door, and that would tell George how much milk to leave. In hot weather, we would place the jugs immediately into crocks of cold water, and hope that the milk would remain useable until the next morning. The milkman sold eggs as well, and I used to love to watch him put a dozen eggs into a paper bag and swing it over and over to twist the top securely. He never dropped any. For much of my childhood we had our own chickens, so Mum seldom had to buy eggs. Pop constructed a walk-in chicken run at the top of the garden, and in there with the chickens lived Pinky the white rabbit. I believe he thought he was a chicken too. When the chickens were fed, Pinky appeared and took his place at the dish with the birds, and they never molested him. They all lived most happily together.

The coal man came once a week - or once a fortnight, I don't remember which, but as every drop of hot water that we had needed to be heated on the kitchen range, the fire had to be kept going all the year round.

Mum never bought greengrocery. What Pop couldn't supply from the garden, we went without. He did very well and supplied us with potatoes, carrots, parsnips, peas, broad and runner beans and every kind of greens. He also cultivated a long raspberry row and a huge bed of rhubarb, as well as gooseberry and black, red and white currant bushes. It was a matter of great pride to him on a summer Sunday, to be able to see on his dinner plate anything up to seven different vegetables that had come fresh that morning from his garden. For a short time however, there was a chappie who called every Sunday afternoon, just about at tea-time, and he sold the more exotic fruit so, if he was in a beneficent mood, Pop would buy a large bunch of bananas or some oranges or grapes as a special Sunday treat. Mum never bought any of those things except at Christmas, unless someone was in hospital, when she would take them grapes.

The grocer was the only tradesman who was not local. Mum bought her groceries from the International Stores in Tunbridge Wells. Every Friday a lad would come round on a bicycle and collect Mum's order, and on Saturday the goods would be delivered on the van. This meant that Mum ordered only what she wanted and was not seduced into buying 'extras.' Sometimes they had special offers, which she would buy if she thought they were good value for money. Once they offered a good sized glass vase filled with raspberry jam, and she bought two of those. The vases remained in service for years. Otherwise she just bought basics:- tea, brown and white sugar, flour - both plain and self-raising, cheese, the 'mouse-trap' variety, bacon if she planned to make a bacon pudding for dinner during the week, a packet of semi-sweet biscuits, a packet of cream crackers, cake fruit which she would have to wash and dry thoroughly before it could be used, butter - she would never eat margarine, a few tins of sardines or pilchards, soap-flakes for washing up and hard Fairy soap for the washing. This hard soap she would leave to get even harder before she would use it, to make it go further.

Monday was washing day, and on that day the copper fire would be lit. Pop usually filled the copper for her before he went to work, and it would provide enough boiling hot water, with several refills, for her to do all her washing and boil up her sheets and pillow cases and other boilable items. The other time when the copper fire was lit was on bath nights, when her big tin bath would be placed in front of the copper fire and, one by one, we children would be put in it. It was a cosy, comfortable way to have a bath, even when we grew so much that we could only fit in with difficulty. The thing that spoilt my bath time, was the dreadful knowledge that underneath the scullery floor there was supposed to be a filled-in well, and I was terrified that the floor would give way and I would fall into it. Once, when I was very little, we visited someone we called Granny Pooley. She was old and while Mum was chatting to her, we children were sent to play in the garden. We had a lovely time in an overgrown corner until an anguished shout from the house told us to come indoors at once. We were shaken and yelled at,

'Don't you realise that there's a well in that corner? You could have fallen in and never been seen again.' How the heck were we supposed to know?

I realise now, how frightened the grown-ups were at the time, and how much they blamed themselves for not being more vigilant, but that is where my fear of wells began. Apart from that, there was a well in our flower garden, and every few years we would suddenly become the reluctant owners of a great hole about three feet deep. Pop would fill it up with garden waste and anything else that came to hand, until it was level with the surrounding soil. I figured that, if that well dropped three feet every few years, then the one in the scullery, which had been covered over since the year dot, must be fathoms deep by now. I remained apprehensive about that scullery floor till we moved out of the house in 1958.

The top of the copper came in very useful to put things on, and sometimes you could barely see it for the things that were piled on it. Mum was crafty, and if she thought our insides needed a bit of help, she would mix up some brimstone and treacle in her handleless Wedgwood jug, and leave it on the copper. She never dosed us with it, and never told us it was there, but she knew we would steal a spoonful every time we went through the scullery - using the spoon that was so conveniently left in it - and the excitement of making sure we weren't caught added to the good it undoubtedly did us.

Mum never attempted to do her washing and ironing on the same day. By the time she had pegged the last load of wet clothes on to the line to dry, the day was far advanced and she was exhausted. She aimed to get the first lineful out as early as possible so that it had a chance to dry before the next lot was ready. She was helped considerably by the fact that she had a mangle - two large rollers driven by a great wheel that was turned by a handle. If we children were at home, one of us would be detailed to turn the mangle, and it was quite hard work. All the wet washing was put through the mangle, and the last possible drop of superfluous water was wrung out of it. When the sheets were dry and folded, they were mangled instead of being ironed. It always amused me that wet clothes were 'wrung' through the 'wringer' and dry ones were 'mangled' through the 'mangle,' but the same machine did both jobs.

Ironing was another chore. Mum needed to have a good fire in the kitchen range, so in hot weather it was murder. She had three flat-irons, and she had one upended in front of the fire and one keeping warm on top while she was using the third. When the one she was using cooled down, she put it on top of the stove, moved the one that was there down to the front of the fire and took the one that was there to use. To test if the iron was hot enough to use, she either spat on it to see how quickly it sizzled dry or she licked her finger and just touched it for the same reaction - you had to be quick to get away with that one - or she held it up close to her face and judged the amount of heat that emanated from it. Actually Mum quite liked ironing, unlike this daughter who hates it.

She did her ironing on the kitchen table, which she covered with two layers of blanket and a piece of sheeting. This material collectively was referred to as the ironing cloth. When not in use, the ironing cloth was kept rolled up on the corner of the stairs. Our stairs were completely enclosed, with a door at the bottom that opened into the living room, and the bend at the bottom was used as a mini cloakroom. There were hooks and nails in the wooden panelling to hang coats on, and a shelf in the actual wall above them to put things on. More often than not, we just tossed everything on top of the ironing cloth in the corner of the stairs, and many lost treasures came to light when Mum did the ironing!

At various times in my life, I took to sleep-walking, and many's the time I have woken up to find myself curled up on the ironing cloth. Whether I walked down to it or fell I don't know, but I suspect the latter.

Another job Mum enjoyed doing was cleaning windows, and we never had a dirty window in our house. I hang my head in shame, but I comfort myself with the thought that she didn't have to remove a heavy pane of double glazing before she could start! As I think I have mentioned elsewhere, Mum was a parlour-maid before she was married and she liked glass to shine. It wasn't easy to clean the outside of the bedroom windows, and when we were older, Ella would sit on the window-sill with her legs in the bedroom and all the rest of her hanging outside, while I sat on the floor inside holding on to her legs for dear life. If I had relaxed my hold for an instant she would have crashed to the ground.

56

Most of our ailments and injuries were dealt with by Mum's own medicaments. Brimstone and treacle was a good standby, although Pop favoured senna-pods and used to bring us each a dose on Sunday morning which we had to drink, come hell or high water, before we could have our cup of tea. I hated the stuff and fought against every mouthful, in spite of his assurances that it had no taste at all. When we had sore throats Mum made a preparation called butter-sugar. She put brown sugar and butter into the Wedgwood jug and added a few things that we knew nothing about, and probably wouldn't have swallowed if we had known, though I am sure that lemon juice was one of them. Then she mixed them all together and again left the jug on the copper for us to steal the contents.

Being very active, outdoor children, we suffered the usual amount of cuts and bruises which were all treated with Mum's green ointment. I never knew what went into it apart from bees-wax, but she made pots and pots of it at a time, and it smelt as if it was doing you a lot of good. Her most memorable concoction was her cough mixture. She would put a pound of black treacle into her big white jug and pour boiling water on to it, I don't know how much, I would guess it was a quart. Into that she would pour the contents of two small bottles, a mixture of, among other things, laudanum, paregoric, syrup of squills, epicacuana wine, eucalyptus - I forget what else - and stir it all together. The resultant brew was delicious and effective. She kept it in coffee bottles on the shelf in the kitchen, and when we had colds we were given an egg-cupful after meals. Unfortunately, it was too delicious, and we were never satisfied with one dose. We usually managed to sneak a second one and, if we could, we just tipped up the bottle. One day the milkman came to the door with a streaming cold so Mum gave him a bottle with strict instructions as to dosage. Like us, he found the stuff irresistible and finished the bottle before he finished his round. When I think of the gallons of that mixture that we children got through, it seems ridiculous that nowadays it would be impossible to make it as one, at least, of the ingredients is listed as a poison, and cannot be bought over the counter.

Funnily enough I met a lady recently, older than myself, whose mother also had the recipe. She understood that her mother was given it by gypsies. I never knew where Mum got her recipe from. One thing is for sure, Pop was not amused when I picked up the wrong bottle and made him a cup of coffee, complete with milk and sweetener, from cough mixture instead of Camp coffee.

I have touched on various aspects of Christmas from time to time, so I think I had better put it into the picture properly. In the days before freezers and fridges, much of the preparation for Christmas food had to be left to the last minute. Mum paid into a couple of Christmas clubs, one of which was actually with her grocer, and with that money she bought icing sugar, cake fruit, candied peel, dates, figs and suchlike seasonal goodies. She made her own mincemeat, and we children were set to work cutting up raisins, sultanas and peel, which came in large pieces coated in candy sugar. We grew very tired of the job but that didn't save us.
'You'll enjoy eating the mince pies and the cake and pudding,' she used to say, 'so you can do your bit towards making them.' At least we got to eat some of the fruit.

Mum made the Christmas cake and Uncle Frank iced and decorated it, having once worked in a bakery. The puddings boiled on the kitchen range for hours on end. The goose or turkey or whatever was delivered on Christmas Eve and, like as not, Pop had to pluck and truss it - then there were feathers and 'damns' flying everywhere! On Christmas Eve, Mum baked mince pies and got everything ready for the Christmas dinner.

On Christmas morning, we opened our stockings, which Uncle Frank had had a hand in filling, so one year we each had a carefully wrapped piece of coal among the more usual contents.
'How nice of Father Christmas,' said Mum 'to put something in for me. He must know how expensive coal is.' We all solemnly watched as our personal bits of coal burned on the front-room fire. As I had a young sister and a much younger brother, I got away with having a stocking for much longer than I should have done. Mum was afraid I might spill the beans and spoil things for the little ones, but she needn't have worried, I knew when I was on to a good thing!

We all went to Church in the morning. Mum went to the early Communion, and Pop took the rest of us to the service at 11 o'clock. The rest of the day was given up to merriment. The fire was lit in the big duck's nest fireplace in the front room, and paper-chains hung from the ceiling. We had the same paper-chains for years, kept together with pins, paper clips, hair grips, bits of string or cotton and anything else that would make them hold out for another year.

We had our Christmas dinner around 1 o'clock, but about midday, everything came to a solemn stop while the elderberry wine was broached. Mum, like me, refused to drink anything alcoholic on an empty stomach so, with the wine, came another Christmas treat, fancy biscuits. We children had only the merest taste of the wine but we did well on the biscuits. That wine certainly was powerful - more potent than anything you could buy in the shops. I still make elderberry wine in exactly the same way that Mum made it and it is just as potent and just as delicious. It is absolutely my favourite of all drinks, but I have to be very careful or it attacks my elbows, which turn to jelly and ache like fun. With most people it is their knees that feel the effects of strong drink but with me it is my elbows!

Our Christmas dinner was poultry of some sort, with stuffing and bread sauce, roast potatoes and sprouts. The vegetables were from the garden. Then we had a huge Christmas pudding into which Mum had put some silver threepenny bits. In later years, these became obsolete and Mum borrowed some from my collection (which I still have) and Pop bought them back for me. With the pudding went white sauce as Mum didn't like custard with Christmas pudding. Then the men did the washing up.

By the time everything was put to rights and we were all settled in the front room, it was time for the King's speech, after which we had our presents. In the main we had board games and books. The board games kept us busy for the rest of the Christmas period, and the grown-ups forgot their dignity and spent Christmas afternoon and evening playing ludo, snakes and ladders, draughts and chinese chequers with us. I was a complete bookworm and pounced on any books that I received and had read and digested the lot before the school holiday was over. One year, Auntie Annie made us some gloves. It was the only time she ever gave us a Christmas present.

Tea-time was late on Christmas Day but, when Mum gave the signal, the front room table was cleared, a clean white cloth was spread on it and all the usual things brought in - a loaf of bread, a dish of butter (we never had bread and butter spread beforehand but spread each slice as we needed it), cheese, various jams and spreads and, in addition, a huge dish of mince-pies and the Christmas cake. For us the cake was the crowning glory of Christmas. It was a rich fruit cake with the marzipan and royal icing spread thickly and, year after year, the same little snow-babies disported themselves on the top surrounded by the little silver balls that we all loved. We knew that we mustn't have any cake until we had taken the edge off our hunger - hunger! - with more mundane things so when we finally received our slice we scarcely had room for it. Always we removed the icing to save till last, and always by the time we got to it we were too sick to look at it, so there were little bits of icing carefully put away for later on.

There always seemed to be plenty of people around at Christmas, I can't remember a time when we were on our own. Auntie Mary came and Uncle Frank and his current lady friend. We always made a lot of noise and anyone passing by must have thought it was a mad-house. By the time that we were sent off to bed, slightly later than usual, we were exhausted and fell asleep as soon as our heads touched the pillows.

Sometimes, on Boxing morning, the Salvation Army band would come and play carols outside our house. Pop had a great affinity with the Salvation Army and would have joined them, I think, if there had been a group near enough. Anyway he loved band music and sang the carols with them, even if he didn't know the words very well, wearing the pseudo-holy expression which he deemed to be suitable for the occasion.

CHAPTER 7

I think it's time I introduced some of our neighbours. Across the road was a pair of semi-detached cottages, each one of which had a long garden running along the road at the side of the house. The one nearest to us belonged to an old man, Mr. Eagles, and we would often go over and play in his garden. He never minded. I think he liked having us around as long as we didn't get on his vegetables. His dustbin-lid always seemed to be upside-down on the bin, and rain-water used to collect in it. When this happened, we used to 'wash' Ella's doll's clothes and hang them out on his clothes line to dry. We never did any harm and on the whole he never took much notice of us. Then he developed an ugly sore on his bottom lip which got bigger and bigger. Mum said we weren't to go over there any more, and shortly afterwards, he died. I asked why he died and Mum said 'Cancer.' It was the first time I'd ever heard the word. Now there is another house built in what used to be his garden.

In the other semi lived the Lawrence family. Mr Lawrence was a carpenter and cabinet-maker with a shed for a workshop in his field, bang opposite our house. I don't remember very much about him because he died when I was very young. I still possess a cabinet that he made. His wife, known to all and sundry as 'old Emmy,' was a complete dragon of a woman, and kept him firmly under her thumb. Years after his death she remarried, and treated her new husband in exactly the same way. Their son, Maurry, was my big sister's boon companion when they were little, but by the time I came on the scene he was very much a 'big boy' and I was in great awe of him. There was a sort of chalet in their garden where lived a tubby little man named Mr. Chambers. Maurry despised him utterly and always referred to him as 'Daddy Harry' so we did likewise - but not when he was near enough to hear us. Maurry was sometimes heard to remark,
'The way he orders me around, you'd think he was my old man.' The grown-ups used to give knowing grins when they heard him say it. We were still quite young when both of those houses changed hands. The Clarke family moved into Mr. Eagles' house and the Lewises into the other one.

Our house was built so that the two front doors opened right on to the path that ran beside the road, and our flower garden was beside the house, separated from the path by a fairly elegant fence. Beyond the garden was another pair of semis, built end-on to the road. Incidentally, these cottages, now made into one 'des res,' have recently changed hands for a quarter of a million pounds. In the one furthest from the road lived 'Woogy' and 'Uncle Dicker.' Uncle Dicker had a horse and trap which he kept in a field near the tree-trunk. At weekends he would drive up to the gate, Woogy would climb aboard and off they would go. He was a little round man, and she was a bony, angular woman crippled with arthritis. She was a good friend to all of us, and we could run in and out of her house as we liked - unless she caught us nicking her pears when she would tell Mum and it would mean the stick. It didn't stop us though. When Uncle Dicker was suffering his last illness, they had their bed brought down into their front room, as she was completely unable to climb the stairs to care for him. He was almost immobile and extremely bad-tempered. This bad temper really got to her, and we discovered that, before she settled down for the night, she removed his braces from the bed-post in case he got up in the night and strangled her with them.

When Nellie, and her family were evicted from their first home, which was a tied cottage, they came back home to Mum, but our house couldn't comfortably accommodate all five of them so Nellie, Len and the new baby slept at Woogy's and the two girls stayed with us. Each morning, Nellie would come over to see to her two little daughters, leaving the baby asleep in his cot. When he woke up Woogy would put a sheet of newspaper in her front window and Nellie would go over and get him.

When Woogy and Uncle Dicker died, their house was take over by Peter and Ella Bateup. Ella's father, Mr. Prior, had bought Mr. Lawrence's field and turned it into a market garden - thereby stopping for ever our games there and our access to the chestnut trees and the wood beyond the field. Peter and Ella helped with the market garden and took it over when the old man died. They were friendly, salt-of-the-earth people, and sometimes I went over and helped to plant out seedlings or pick fruit or flowers for them. They sold fruit and vegetables as well as plants and flowers and were very handy for us, although Pop kept us supplied with practically all the vegetables we needed from his garden and allotment.

In the other house lived 'Old Tick.' He had once had a wife, but she left him and he remained alone for years. Again, we ran in and out of his house as we liked. He had a fascinating little workroom with a ship in a bottle, a miniature house and garden in a glass case and many other treasures. He mended clocks and watches, and had one of those magnifying glasses that you almost screw into your eye. He was the caretaker for the Methodist Chapel, so when he was in there cleaning we went in with him to play. He wasn't a religious man, so he never minded if we played in and out of the pews. Mum would have had forty fits if she'd known. He also did gardening for the big house behind our gardens, so we played there when he was working. The two old ladies who lived there never seemed to mind, but again, we never did any harm and old people often enjoy the sound of children playing happily.

We had to be careful because his temper was uncertain, and he would suddenly round on us and send us home. He had a tuft of white violets growing under his doorstep, and yellow musk and ivy-leafed toadflax along the side of the house. Mum didn't approve of him and didn't like him, but she felt sorry for him - folk said that he was shell-shocked in the war (14-18) - so at Christmas she always sent him along a few hot mince pies. She would have approved even less if she had seen him blow his nose with his finger tips straight on to the floor. We discovered that many of our friends weren't allowed to come and play with us because we lived near that 'horrible old man.' Ella had a quick temper, and one day, when he was teasing her, he called her a spitfire and chanted,
'Spitfire, spitfire, spitfire, SPIT' so she did - right at him - and from then on he became our bitterest enemy. It didn't worry us one little bit which only angered him more. His animosity showed itself in many petty little ways. I was walking down the hill one day as he was coming up. He very pointedly crossed over the road and 'walked by on the other side,' gazing fixedly into the hedge as he did so. Another time, Pop was coming out of the forge in the village and met him coming in. Pop held the door open for him to go through, but he let Pop get out then he closed the door, latched it, reopened it and went through. On the whole we found the situation very amusing, and made up weird and wonderful stories of what he might do 'if.....'

During the war another lady took up residence with him. She was a good hearted homely sort of body and she remained with him until he died. How she put up with him I'll never know, but I think he had to do as he was told.

In a cottage by the cross-roads lived Miss Dunk. She was a misshapen little lady who would chase us off if we were playing on the railings outside her house. Quite possibly she feared we would hurt ourselves. Anyway, there were plenty more railings to play on, so we kept away most of the time. We didn't deliberately set out to upset people. For many years she was the secretary of the WI, and when she retired they gave her some very delicate bone china cups and saucers. At some stage her sister, Mrs. Allwork, moved into the cottage next door to her, which was so minute you barely had room to breathe. She asked Mum if she would launder her sheets for her, and so we got to know her fairly well when we collected and returned them.

One Sunday morning she came along to Mum in great distress, and said she feared something had happened to Jane. She couldn't open her bedroom door and Jane didn't answer when she called. Mum hurried along and found that Miss Dunk had died in the night, and had fallen behind the door. She forced her way into the bedroom, took stock of the situation and then rang the doctor. I can't remember all that transpired, but the end result was that Pop took over the phone and was given implicit instructions on what to do to lay out a dead body, which he then did.

Mrs. Allwork was deeply grateful, and wanted to give Mum something of Jane's as a memento. Mum chose those bone china cups and saucers. I still have them.

Over the cross-roads and down the hill a little way lived the three Miss Wrights, elderly spinsters who used to go past our house every Sunday to church, dressed identically in long grey raincoats, black boots and black hats. We called them the twinsies and the odd twin. They always walked in formation - the twins side by side in front and the odd twin bringing up the rear, and always on the road, never on the path.

I was quite small when the house next door changed tenants. I don't know who divided the pub into two dwellings, but it was done most unfairly. We

64

had eight rooms and a huge cellar - which was on the same level as the rest of the house. They had two rooms downstairs and two up - all much smaller than any of ours.

A widow with her three children moved in and we soon became friends. We never played in each other's houses, but we played outside together all the time. We made camps, dug mines, laid trails and generally played as most kids play. Unlike ours, their garden was completely uncultivated, but it contained an old, gnarled pear tree which regularly produced a huge crop of the most delicious pears I have ever tasted. They were never picked and more of them fell into our garden than theirs. We had to share them with the wasps.

We lived at the top of a hill, and on our side of the road, left as you walked up from the village, was a grass-verged footpath. This rose at a faster rate than the road itself and reached its peak later, so by the time you reached our home there was a three-foot drop from the path to the road. A few yards further on, the drop was fifteen feet or more. In front of our house there was a retaining wall instead of the grass verge, surmounted by a single tubular steel railing set in concrete posts. On the other side of our gate there was no wall, just a grass bank, also surmounted by railings but these were solid iron rails set in wooden posts. We could do anything on these railings and we spent hours upside down on them. We could go over forwards and backwards, hang from knees, crawl along them under or over and swing happily from the path to the road. We had contests, moving along the rails as the bank got higher to see who could tackle the biggest drop. It's a wonder none of us ever broke any bones, but we never did. At its highest point the bank gave way again to a retaining wall which continued - dropping in easy stages - to the cross-roads. Here the contest was to see who could jump from the highest point - or how near to it one could get. Modern parents would have forty fits!

At the other side of the road was a much higher bank with Mr. Lawrence's/Mr. Prior's field at the top. It produced masses of blue and white violets in the spring, and equal masses of wild strawberries in the summer. We loved to climb to the top of this bank by the most difficult route - North Face of the Eiger! and walk along the top which, in summer, was crowned by masses of nettles. Often we managed to hit a ball on to the top of the bank and the game stopped while we struggled to find it. If the search proved fruitless, we would sometimes try to hit another ball in the same way, carefully noting where it landed. Sometimes of course we lost two balls, but, strangely enough, nine times out of ten, it worked - and we often found long-lost balls as well.

I think that here is a good place to introduce Hixie. She lived about two miles away and was Mum's best friend. When Mum and Pop first moved into a home of their own, it was a cottage on the farm where Pop worked, and Hixie lived in another of the cottages. When they moved into the home that I remember, it still belonged to the farm, and Mum was expected to continue working there, even though she now lived two miles away and there was no transport. She refused. Hixie remained her friend and was the kind of friend that few people are lucky enough to find. I can remember her arriving at home one morning when Mum was ill and announcing,
'I've come to do the washing.' She would order us about just as Mum did, and we knew better than to disobey her. She had three sons and a little girl. The youngest boy was two days younger than me and I never let him forget it. He grew up to be a scientist and Mayor of his town. The middle boy was killed at Arnhem. He was a tall ungainly lad with a heart of gold and we missed him terribly. The boys would sometimes come up to play with us on a Saturday, which suited us fine because they were early risers and often arrived before we were up and did most of our jobs for us so that we could get out more quickly.

The cottage in which they lived was set well back from the main road, and had a short flight of stone steps and a long brick path which led to the front door - only no-one ever used the front door. The most usual way in was through the farm gate, skirt round the pig-sties, go across in front of the hay-barn and in through the back door. This led into the scullery, which was a large room with an uneven brick floor and the only water tap in the house. We visited Hixie quite often, as the bus went right past her house, and when we did, we loved being packed off to play with the boys while the two ladies settled down to a good gossip. There were fields to play in, sheds we could wander through, odd little pools and streams of water and a pond. The house was pulled down many years ago and only the flight of stone steps remained to show where once it had been. People were heard to wonder why those steps should be there leading to nothing. Now they are gone too, and the hay-barn, the pig-sties, the oast-house and the other farm buildings have all been converted into private homes - another piece of History gone.

Hixie moved to another farm some two miles or more further away from us, and we didn't see her so often, but we were teenagers by then and were able to cycle over to her house. I was holding her new baby - very much an afterthought - when a doodlebug fell not too far away from the house. After the explosion we rushed outside to see the plume of smoke and were amazed at how small it was. We were so intrigued by this that we failed to notice another one chugging towards us, until its engine cut out. There was never a silence so deafening as the moment when a doodlebug's engine stopped. We all dived indoors for cover but this one brought the ceilings down and we were covered in plaster.

Hixie remained an important person in my life until she died of cancer in 1985.

Her husband, Uncle Ern, had died eleven years earlier. He was a typical tiller of the soil who seemed to know instinctively what needed to be done, and when, for any plant in his care. No weed ever reared its head in his garden. He usually managed to get home for his dinner at midday, and when he had eaten he would spend ten minutes or so hoeing between his vegetables or earthing up his potatoes. His world began and ended with the soil. In his younger days, he had emigrated to New Zealand, but nothing about him suggested that he had ever left the Home Counties, let alone travelled to the Antipodes. I believe that he came back to play his part in the Great War but I am not sure. I never heard him talk about it. I never knew him to hurry either. Everything he did was done slowly. Even his speech was slow as though he was giving great thought to every word he said - but he wasn't.

When I was grown-up and owned a car we all went to Hastings. I was going off into the town leaving Mum, Hixie and Uncle Ern in deckchairs on the sea-front. Ern took a good look around and spotted the ticket man coming, so he stood looking over the railings at the sea until he was safely past and then he sat down. When I returned he was full of how clever he'd been, and how stupid the two ladies were to pay 4d each for a chair when they could have been like him and got it for free.

'You know, Ernie,' I said, 'if you were any kind of a gentleman you would pay half of the cost for them. Go on, give them 2d each.'

'Not likely,' he said, 'they should have been wide awake like me.' But some time later he sidled up to Mum and said,

'Here you are Lucy, I reckon it's only fair if I pay half of your chair money. I've given 2d to the wife.' and he put 2d into her hand. He never woke up to the fact that he had actually paid 4d while they had paid 2d each.

During that afternoon Hixie had done some shopping and was carrying a heavy bag along with her.

'Come on Ernie,' I said, 'surely you aren't going to let her carry that bag. That's a man's job.'

'No, that's alright' said Hixie, 'I can manage. The bag's heavy.'

'No, give it to me. I'll take it.' said Ernie, and he did.

A few minutes later I heard him saying to Hixie,

'You were right Else, it is heavy. Take it back will you.' and she did.

When my father died, we offered Ernie his almost brand new trilby hat, and were rather taken aback by his response.

'Frank only wore his hat a couple of times.' said Mum, 'Would you like to have it?'

'No, I jolly well wouldn't.' he answered.

'Oh, sorry.' said Mum apologetically.

'Do you want to know why?' he said, 'I'll show you.'

He put the hat on. It was quite obviously several sizes too large for him and looked absolutely ridiculous.

'Frank's head was always a lot bigger than mine.' he said, when the laughter had died down. 'So thanks all the same, but no thanks.'

For as long as I could remember, Hixie had a lodger, a little gnome-like man called Pots. His name was, I believe, Moore but he had been a travelling tinker before he retired and so he was always called Pots, usually with the prefix 'old.' He rode everywhere on his trusty bike, and quite often turned up at our house with messages from Hixie. He viewed with disfavour Mum's new knives and offered to sharpen them for her. Very avante-guarde those knives were, with stainless steel blades and bone handles - at least it looked like bone. Mum was horrified when he tied her six knives on to the carrier of his bike.

'Let me find something to wrap them in.' she said, 'They could easily fall off and get lost.'

'Stop fussing.' he said, 'they are perfectly safe.' but when he got them home there were only five. He bought Mum another one but it wasn't quite the same so Mum kept the odd one as 'her' knife and used it until she died. I still have that knife, and four of the original six. I wonder what happened to the other one?

Pots ordered the boys about much more than their father did, but they took no notice of him at all - any more than they did of their father. It was Hixie who ruled the roost and her word was law.

My father died early on a Sunday morning in the middle of March in 1957. As soon as she heard the news Hixie arrived, and saw her duty to be protecting Mum and me. We had had a terrible night, as Pop had suffered a stroke on the previous day, and we had taken turns to watch over him all night until he died at about 6 am. We were both exhausted, and completely unable to cope with the people who came to offer condolences. Hixie more or less took charge, tactfully getting rid of people when she considered it wise, and then ordering us off to bed before going home herself. We had several aunts and honorary aunts, but no-one outside the immediate family was more important to us than Hixie.

CHAPTER 8

The heart of our house was the kitchen, and, as the house was built into the slope of the hill, the kitchen window, which was about four feet from the floor on the inside, was actually at ground level outside. Like all the other downstairs rooms in the house, the kitchen had a concrete floor. Mum put down strips of coconut matting and polished the bits in between with a red stone polish. The kitchen range was situated across one corner, and provided all the heat in the house, unless the front room fire was lit. The kitchen fire was always alight, and kettles sat on the top, permanently heating up, and saucepans for vegetables joined them when needed. The oven was always hot, too, so that Mum did a lot of baking. The mantelpiece above the fireplace held the tea tin, two biscuit tins, a few assorted vases and ornaments, the big American clock and the stick! On the wall either side of the clock were enlarged photographs, in brown wooden frames, of Mum's parents.

There was one huge table in the middle of the room which was covered permanently with American cloth - similar to plastic but much thicker with a soft backing to it. On this table, Mum would put her machine when she was sewing, her ironing cloth when she was ironing and her mixing bowl and pastry board when she was baking. There was a special groove cut into the underside of the edge so that Pop's knitting machine could be fitted on it with a clamp. It was, in fact, the general work table and also the meal table - except for Sunday tea which we had in the front room.

Mum was fussy about meals. The table was covered with a decent tablecloth, usually white with a coloured border, and we all sat down together in our own places. The centre of one of the long sides was the place for the tea-tray or the serving dish depending on which meal it was. Mum always sat on the right hand side of the tray in the position nearest the fire, and on the other side of the tray, Pop sat in a chair with arms, which meant that he was always sideways on to the table. We girls sat opposite them and our brother was at the short end by Mum, which put him in a perfect position for kicking us under the table, which he did with great regularity.

At tea-time, the bread, on its wooden bread-board (which I still have), was always placed at the bottom corner of the table, diagonally across from Mum, and the cake, on a glass cake-stand was in the centre behind the tea-tray.

There was no silly rule about not speaking during meals, and we all chattered away quite happily, as long as we didn't try to speak with food in our mouths. We had to sit there until Mum decided that we could leave the table, when we would gabble
'Thank God for our good dinner. Amen.' which usually came out as 'God.dinner.men.' Then we had to clear away, wash up, put away the crocks and clear off on our own devices. Sometimes, when we were hauled in from some engrossing pastime, we would say we weren't hungry and didn't want any dinner. Then Mum would say
'Well, you can just sit in your places and watch me eat mine.' So that was a non-starter!

When the last meal was finished and the day's work done, Mum put a heavy dark cloth on the table to make the room look less like a kitchen and more like a sitting room. In the evenings, in winter, we would use one end of the table for a game of whist.

The kitchen had four doors leading out of it, one into the scullery and thence to the back door, one to the stairs, one to the front room and the front door, and one into what was known as the pantry and so to the external door we always used.

In this room were food safes for storing food, crocks for wine making and cupboards for storing anything that didn't have a home anywhere else. We kept our bicycles in there too - never less than three of them. When Granny died and Uncle Ted came to live with us, be brought with him Granny's huge kitchen dresser which, from our point of view, was very useful, as we rolled all our balls under it out of the way. We never knew how many were there, and when we wanted one we swung a long stick to and fro under the dresser until a ball came rolling out. There was a large, low cupboard, known as the red cupboard, in which Mum kept all her jam, jars and jars of it, and her bottled fruit. There was a corner cupboard which reached up to the ceiling in which Mum kept all the things that she didn't use very often.

In front of that were crocks, the huge bread crock, the tiny butter crock and crocks full of waterglass eggs and salted runner beans.

The scullery at the back of the house was even deeper under the ground than the kitchen, and the one sink and tap in the house were directly under the window, so if you wanted to clean or open the window you had to stand on a chair.

Beside the sink was a large table-like article always known as the block, and in the corner between that and the copper was the general dumping ground. Opposite the copper was the mangle, another good place for dumping things when it wasn't in use, and against the other wall, between the scullery door and the back door, was the kneading trough where Mum kept all her tea-cloths and other useful bits of cloth.

The front room was kept for Sundays and Christmas. Just like the kitchen it had a fireplace across one corner of the room, in fact, the two grates backed each other. Above it on the mantelpiece were various ornaments - nothing of any value apart from sentiment - and a china clock that didn't go but looked pretty. There was a corner cupboard opposite it on which stood the clock that did go, a black marble one, and a stuffed red squirrel holding a nut. Along the wall beside that cupboard was a leather sofa - heaven only knows where Pop got that - and above it, hanging on the wall, was a glass fronted case with a stuffed kingfisher in it. There was a small table under the window and a large gate-legged table in the centre of the room.

Mum had always pined for a three piece suite, and when her children were no longer of a destructive age, she treated herself to one. Then the leaves of the table were let down, the table was placed under the window and the room truly became a sitting-room which was used more often, especially in summer.

When I was very small, the only lighting in the house came from an oil lamp and candles, then the electricity company advertised a package deal, which gave six lights and all the fittings for a price which the parents felt they could afford. They had lights put in the kitchen, the front room, the pantry, the two front bedrooms and on the stairs. Then Uncle Frank got to work and by using double fittings and heaven knows what else he rigged up lights for the scullery and the other two bedrooms. Mum then had an electric iron which she fitted into the kitchen light socket.

We had four bedrooms, two at the front and two at the back. The two on the left of the landing were each reached by means of two steps. The front one on the left, the only one that boasted a fire-place, was the parents' room. As well as the big double bed, it contained a large chest-of-drawers, which I still use, a large wooden chest for clothes, which I also have, another chest which held Pop's clothes, a wardrobe, a wash-stand with a basin and jug, and various chairs. The other front bedroom was the spare room for visitors, until we got older when it became our room, that is Ella and me. Before that, and before Nellie left home to go into service, we all three shared a double bed in the back room on the left of the landing, which was over the kitchen. It also had the advantage of being separated from the parents' room by nothing more substantial than a wooden partition, so Mum could hear me when I went sleep-walking.

The other back room was mostly unused. It was small, and the walls were in such a bad condition that in some places you could see right to the outside. When Uncle Ted came to live with us, Mum made the room habitable and that was his room and it was there that he died. After his death, we children were scared to go in there for a long time, but it eventually became my brother's room until we moved into the front room and he had ours. When it was empty, it was a useful place for storing apples, pears and other fruits.

All the doors in the kitchen and front room had hand-made mats on the floor in front of them, which my father made by threading strips of material on to rectangles of sacking - and very good they were too. The bedroom doors all had them, and there were two huge ones used as hearthrugs in front of the fires in the kitchen and the front room. I made one once, it was really hard work. Mind you, we children had the job of cutting up the material into strips. We weren't allowed to use any of Mum's good scissors, and when mat-making was in progress I had permanently blistered hands.

Another job that turned up in the winter was 'brutting' potatoes. Pop had an allotment as well as his garden and he grew enough potatoes to last us through the winter. These would be stored in wooden barrels and tubs in the cellar and in due course would begin sprouting. When this happened, we had to tip out all the potatoes and break off the shoots, so that they did not take all the goodness out of the potatoes. It was a long, boring, tedious job and we hated it.

The allotment was about three-quarters of a mile away, opposite the school. The biggest problem was getting the produce home in the days before we had a car. Pop would take his tradesman's bike and a supply of sacks - and it was absolutely inevitable that one or more of the sacks would have a hole in it. We had to help push the bike, which was completely loaded down, and the journey was all uphill. First one potato, then another, would fall through a hole in the sack. We would collect up the strays and put them back, Pop would tie a piece of string round the hole and we would continue the journey. Sometimes a whole sack would collapse, and we had to chase potatoes all the way back down the road. The 'damns' would come thick and fast, and Pop would vow never to plant potatoes in the allotment again, but he always did, and we went through the same performance year after year.

That road has another rueful memory for me. Walking home from school one day, I saw Uncle Frank's blue Jowett half way up the hill. I ran up, hoping to get a ride home, but the car wouldn't go, and he was waiting there in the hope that the home-going schoolchildren would give him a push - which they all happily did. I was very small, but I helped push from the back, all the time busily telling everyone who would listen,
'This is my uncle's car. When the car starts he'll give me a ride home.'
Suddenly he let in the clutch, the engine started, the car took off up the hill and I fell flat on my face. When I got home, with scuffed knees and blood all over my face - crying, limping and absolutely miserable, he hadn't even realised that I had been there.

Uncle Frank was my mother's young brother, almost twenty years her junior, and he sort of lived with us until he married. At one time, he was in the regular army, and this tall, khaki-clad figure would appear every now and again. After he was demobbed, he was a permanent fixture, rather like a big brother only decidedly more bossy. One task that seemed to be allotted to him was to cut our hair. My sisters had hair that was parted on the side and held back away from their eyes with hair-grips or slides, but for some reason I had a fringe. Looking back, I really can't think why Mum did that to me. My features and colouring were very different from the other two anyway, and the fringe only made it worse. Very few people ever thought we were sisters. My hair didn't look bad when it was parted neatly in the centre and combed tidily, but that was someone else's responsibility, not mine, and more often than not it rose to a sort of point at the top of my head - which nowadays would probably start a whole new fashion - and then hung where it fell.

Cutting my hair vied with Pop mending shoes or knitting socks in the number of swearwords it produced. As he attacked my fringe the bits of hair fell onto my face and tickled. I put up with it as long as I could and then carefully brushed them away. This invariably meant that the scissors slewed upwards, ruining the nice straight line he had been carefully following. I would get my knuckles rapped or my ears boxed - or both - and he would start again. I always ended up in tears with sore ears and/or knuckles and a fringe that was so short as to be hardly worthy of the name.

When I had a very painful whitlow on my thumb, it was Uncle Frank who came up with the idea of putting pennies in the bottom of a basinful of very hot water, and coaxing me to see how many I could get out. Mind you, when I got them all out he put them all back in some more hot water and I had to start again, which I thought grossly unfair. I think I got to keep a few of them, but knowing Uncle Frank's lifelong attitude to money, I'm pretty sure I didn't get them all.

He had a succession of girl-friends whom we had to call Auntie, but none of them lasted very long. I vaguely remember Auntie Kath. Then came Auntie Florrie whom he eventually married. She worked in a draper's shop in the town, and she came over to us every Wednesday, which was early closing day. From her we received quite exciting presents, all bought from the shop - pretty nighties, fancy umbrellas, socks and gloves. At this time Uncle worked in a local garage, and Auntie's family didn't think he was much of a catch. 'Just a dirty little garage boy' was how they described him, but Auntie was perfectly happy with him, and they remained happy together until his death in 1990.

They married in the Spring and we were all bridesmaids. Nellie and our cousin, Joyce, wore plain blue dresses, little Dutch caps and carried daffodils. Ella and I wore similar dresses made in a blue floral material, little lace caps and we carried primroses, which we had picked in the woods the day before. I hated that dress because it was blue. I still dislike blue and I never wear it. It drains every bit of colour out of me and makes me look dead. When we were small, we often were given similar things differing only in colour - egg-cups, jumpers, mugs, gloves and socks. I always had red, one sister had blue and the other green. Their colours were interchangeable but mine was always red.

My mother was the middle one of three sisters, who were all well into their teens before their little brother was born. Her younger sister, Nellie, died a few weeks after her second child was born, long before Mum herself was married. The baby, a girl hastily christened and named Nora, died too. Mum told me once that it was just too pretty to live. So my sister Nellie got her name from Mum's much-loved lost sister, and I was named after the dead child. If Mum hoped that I would inherit the prettiness, she must have been sadly disappointed. I can just remember Lucy Brice, the other daughter, who visited us now and again. She died of T.B. while I was still very young.

Mum's other sister was Auntie Bessie, who was married to Uncle Walter and lived in Broadstairs. They had two daughters, Joan and Joyce. Joyce was about the same age as Nellie, and Joan was five years older. She seemed very grown-up and remote to Ella and me at the time, but she became a most important person in my life, and I am still reeling from the shock of her very recent and sudden death at the age of 76. We used to go to visit Auntie Bessie, and when I was seven, I stayed with her for seven weeks and went to school in Broadstairs.

While Uncle Frank worked in a garage, on one or two occasions he hired one of their cars, and took the whole lot of us down to East Kent, to let Mum visit her old haunts, and see her old friends. We used to stop at Sturry, where she grew up, Westbere, where she had friends, and then go on to Broadstairs. It was always a wonderful day for us, spoilt only by the fact that I was incurably travel sick, so Mum always provided herself with armfuls of towels, and the car had to make several unscheduled stops.

76

For almost as long as I could remember, Uncle Walter was 'not well' - ulcers or something. Before that, he had been a painter and decorator, and also a fireman. He hated anyone to be happy, and could usually think of something to say or do to spoil things. We called him our miserable uncle. He ate practically nothing, and would hold one very thin slice from a small loaf over the sugar basin, while he lightly dusted it with sugar. That was his evening meal. Auntie Bessie rode around on a bicycle which he hated. He tried to discourage her by telling her,

'You're breaking the law by riding that thing. It hasn't any lights.'

'But I never use it after dark.' she protested.

'That doesn't make any difference,' he said. 'If the police see you in the daylight with no lights, they'll know that if you do go out after dark, you'll be breaking the law, and they'll have you, just in case.' Luckily, she didn't believe him and went on riding her bike for as long as she could.

My father was the youngest son, though he had a younger sister, of a large family. When he was born, his mother was told that she would never rear him, he was so puny and feeble and miserable. The doctor gave him less than a year. He died at the age of 63. Of his brothers, there was Uncle Herbert, who had a butcher's shop in Dover. He cleaned up on the black market in the war and then did jobbing gardening for a local vicar, became rather noisily converted and turned into a true Holy Joe. He had two children, Roy and Edna. His wife, Auntie Laurie was a born complainer. We weren't keen on her at all but we had very little contact with them so it didn't worry us overmuch.

Uncle Herbert outlived Pop by a few years, and in the last years of his life he took to riding a little pop-pop motor-cycle, and he came to visit us on the wretched thing. He had stayed a night or two with Auntie Annie in Haywards Heath, and was calling on us on his way back to Dover. He got himself safely into Tunbridge Wells, and then couldn't remember how to get out. Almost as soon as he realised his predicament, he spotted a policeman on the opposite side of the road, so he went over to ask the way. The policeman shook his head sadly and said to him.

'You know Dad, you really mustn't do that.'

'Do what?'

'Come across the road like that.'

'Well, I wanted to know the way.'

'Yes, but you swung across the road without looking to see if it was safe.'
'Well I had to, didn't I or I'd have gone right past you.'
'But you didn't signal that you were going to come across.'
'I didn't have time for that. I only just saw you in time as it was.'
'But supposing there had been a car coming along to overtake you.'
'Oh, that's his worry not mine. I can't help his troubles.'
I think the policeman gave up in despair!
'Silly young pup.' was Uncle's verdict when he told us about it. I can't think what they're recruiting into the police these days. No common sense at all!'

When it was time for him to leave us, he hit another snag. His little motor-bike didn't feel inclined to start on a steep hill so my brother rode down the hill a little way to get it going and then swung round and came back up to where the old man was waiting. They quickly changed places and he was off - straight up the hill and over the dangerous cross-roads at the top - without a glance either to right or left. How he got home safely we never knew.

After his wife died, he was watched over by a kindly neighbour who did his washing and various other small tasks for him.
'How much do you pay her?' Auntie Annie once asked him.
'Oh, I don't pay her.' he answered. 'She'd be offended if I suggested such a thing.'
'Are you sure?' asked Auntie. 'Have you ever asked her?'
'No, but she does alright. I let her have cabbages and things from my allotment.' he said.
'Oh, well, I expect she appreciates them.' was Auntie's comment.
'I should jolly well hope she does.' he spluttered, 'I don't charge her anything like shop prices for them.'

I can't remember when he died, but I know that at one point, he fell out of a tree in the vicarage garden, which didn't help matters a lot.

Uncle Les was a policeman in Blackheath. We saw him, Auntie Thirza and son Jack now and again when they 'visited the old place.' Uncle Will lived nearby, and dropped in whenever he was passing, though we seldom saw Auntie Rose who was a dedicated invalid and needed constant attention.

Needless to say, she outlived her worn-out husband by about a year. They had several sons and one daughter.

Uncle Ted was Pop's eldest brother. He had a speech defect and 'couldn't talk plain' as they said. I was told he had no roof to his mouth, but I find that hard to believe. We all understood him perfectly because we knew which letters he couldn't pronounce.
'Don't do dat - you nauddy dirl - you'll tut yourdelf. Oh dutty, did you tut your tinder?' and the classic,
'Well, if tod ain't twearin, then tod it.'

He and Grandad rode everywhere on tricycles. When the grandparents celebrated their diamond wedding, the local press latched on to those trikes and tried to make out that Granny rode one too. I don't know how many people it took to hoist her up on to the saddle and hold her there - she was a hefty woman - but they got their picture.

We went down to Granny's a lot. Nowadays it would be a five minute run in the car, but then it was a ten minute bus journey followed by a twenty minute walk. There were only four buses a day, so if you misjudged your timing on the return journey, you walked all the way.

Granny lived in a farm cottage with a tiny front garden in which she grew hyacinths - she called them 'arrasens' - and along the side of the house were masses and masses of blue violets, which I loved. Pop took a plant or two of them up to home and they spread like wildfire. Nellie took some from home for her garden, and later gave some to me, and they have flourished in my garden ever since. I like to think that I have some of Grannie's violets. Grandad had a huge vegetable garden at the side of the house. From the garden, you could climb a stile and be in an apple orchard, where sheep roamed. There was a pond in one corner of it, and great excitement occurred one day when a horse and wagon got into it and couldn't get out. Many years later one of Mum's friends, Louie, drowned herself in that pond. Mum had been to see her the previous day, and, in passing, had admired a glass dish that happened to be on the table.
'If you like it Luce, you have it.' she said, and wouldn't take no for an answer. Mum felt very guilty about taking it, but when the sad news broke

the next day she understood. I still have that glass dish. It is one of my treasures.

A little single track branch railway line ran nearby, and crossed the farm road at a level crossing. When the occasional car came down the road to find the gates closed, the driver had to sound his horn and wait for someone in Granny's house to hear and then walk the two-to-three hundred yards to the gate to open it. Life was more leisurely in those days.

There was one occasion when a crowd of noisy hop-pickers chose to make a fuss about the length of time it took to get the gate open, and the situation looked as though it could develop into something nasty. As it happened, Uncle Les was visiting his mother, so he strolled up to investigate. The trouble-makers were quite happy to have someone else to have a go at - until he showed them his warrant card. Then the tone changed abruptly.
'Cor, look at this. He's a London bobby. Fancy finding a London bobby in this God-forsaken place. Now we'll get fair treatment.'
'Right, that'll do.' said Uncle Les. 'Get yourselves off home.' and they trotted off as meekly as lambs.

Granny's house had two rooms downstairs, the living room and the scullery. In the corner of the scullery was a cluster of long-handled brooms, mops and various other things. Granny had a gramophone, with a huge horn for a loudspeaker, and I was terrified of it. When I saw someone fixing up the horn and preparing to wind the thing up, I went blind and deaf with sheer terror. All the grown-ups thought it was funny and a good way of teasing me. I used to shout 'No.....no,' and run from one to another hoping to find someone who would take me seriously, but everyone said, 'Don't be silly. It can't hurt you.' One day I ran out of the room and into the scullery. I crawled behind all those brooms and things and put my hands over my ears. It was like a secure little wigwam. I heard them calling me but I didn't answer. None of them had taken any notice of my fears, not even my adored Mum. I heard the beginnings of panic and then shouting. People were running in and out, and I heard Pop shout 'I'm going to look in the pond.' They must have been really worried. I can't remember who found me, but I can remember Mum hugging me. They never teased me with that gramophone again, and it was a long time before I became reconciled to it.

I remember eating apple pudding with tinned cream at Granny's. I hadn't tasted tinned cream before. She put cloves in the pudding too. Later on when we visited her, she was ill in bed. I read to her and she gave me a little doggy brooch. She died when I was eleven. She fell down the stairs, but she was dead before she fell. They left it to Auntie Florrie to tell us. She chose the time when she was brushing our hair ready for school and then she whispered,

'Granny's gone to brighter places.' We knew already that she was dead, because we'd been aware of a certain kerfuffle before we'd actually got dressed, and when Pop came in, after he'd been to the station for his fish, he'd exclaimed,

'Dead! My mother!' so Auntie really needn't have bothered. Later we heard someone say, 'She was the best one to tell them,' but we all agreed that Mum would have made a better job of it. It didn't upset us anyway. She wasn't a very loveable character. After her funeral, Grandad went to live with Auntie Annie, his only daughter, and Uncle Ted came to live with us.

Auntie Annie was a real auntie to us. Married to Uncle Alex they had one son, Cecil, who was about the same age as Nellie. Auntie Annie was the family link, keeping in contact with all her brothers. Several times, singly and together, we went to her for a couple of weeks holiday, firstly at Ardingly and then Haywards Heath.

Uncle Ted lived with us for about two years. He worked on a local farm and he rode to and fro on his trike. My brother, an irreverent youngster, noticed that Teddy, as we often called him, always dismounted at the cross-roads and walked round the corner. That particular angle of the cross-roads was less than ninety degrees, about seventy-five, and, either way, one approached on a downward slope and took the seventy-five degree turn to an upward slope. My brother asked him why he didn't ride round.

'Tarn do it - the trite tarn do it.' he said.

'Rubbish, of course it can. Try.' said my brother.

Teddy did try, the trike tipped over and he fell. He dislocated his shoulder and had to spend six weeks in hospital. He never blamed the boy, but he blamed my Mum because she was the one who insisted on his seeing a doctor. My brother, to this day, doesn't feel comfortable about it though. He cannot quite convince himself that Teddy's death was not, albeit indirectly, the result of that accident.

Teddy died just before the war really got spiteful. He caught a chill which rapidly became bronchitis, pleurisy and finally pneumonia. Towards the end he was quite delirious and thought he was picking plums. His legs were climbing the ladder and his arms were reaching out to pick the fruit. They buried him in Paddock Wood churchyard near to his mother. They bought a stone vase inscribed Ted, Rose and Fred to commemorate a brother and sister who had died while young.

I must introduce Auntie Mary. She wasn't really our aunt, but some sort of cousin of Pop's. She was a real character or, to use a more modern idiom, as nutty as a fruit-cake. During my lifetime, she had been 'in service' in various places, but the last place she held was about ten minutes walk from home.

Every Sunday she came to us in the early afternoon and went back to be in by ten. She had Sunday tea with us, and joined in with everything we did. She also came to us on Thursdays, when she had a couple of hours off. On Tuesdays she went to Uncle Will's, and then she walked straight past our house without a sideways glance, and if any of us were playing outside she ignored us, it wasn't 'our' day. This was during the war, and she usually took with her to Uncle Will's some offering, a packet of tea, some butter or cheese, 'to help the rations.' Uncle Will and all his sons worked on the farm and received agricultural rations - extra cheese, butter, margarine, sugar and other bits and bobs, but she felt it was wrong if her one cup of tea and slice of bread and butter came out of their rations. To Mum she brought nothing at all. She regarded our house as home, so it was Mum's duty to feed her as and when.

At one time she worked in Hildenborough, but she still came to us regularly every Sunday. She caught a train to Paddock Wood station and then walked the two miles to our house. She would set off quite happily, just before nine, to catch a train to get her back in time. Winter or summer, dark or light, wet or fine, storm, gale - nothing ever upset her routine. One very snowy day we didn't expect her, but she turned up, a bit late, plodding through the snow. It went on snowing, and conditions were very dodgy so Mum tried to persuade her to stay overnight, but she wouldn't hear of it.

'I got here alright, didn't I?' she said, irritably.

They tied sacking round her shoes in an attempt to stop her slipping, and off she went. About two hours later she was back. She had arrived at the station to find that all trains were cancelled. She took it as a personal insult. If she could walk to the station, then there was no reason why the train couldn't get there.

She attended church regularly every Sunday evening, and she had very fixed ideas about the length of sermon that was acceptable. When she considered that the preacher had spoken for long enough, she took the money for the collection out of her purse. To do this she picked up her bag and opened it, took out her purse, closed her bag and put it back on the floor by her feet. Then she opened her purse, sorted through her money to find the right coin and placed it on the book rest in front of her. Then she closed her purse, picked up her bag, opened it, replaced her purse, closed her bag and put it back on the floor. All this was done very openly with no attempt at discretion, and very few were the preachers who hadn't lost their nerve by then.

She once joined a coach trip to Margate. Mum went and I don't remember who else except that I didn't, so it must have been much later when we were virtually grown-up. When they all met in the coach park for the return journey, Auntie Mary was nowhere to be found. They hunted high and low for her. No-one could remember when they had last seen her. She was renowned for wandering off and getting lost. At last the coach-driver had to leave. He was very apologetic, but he had a deadline for getting out of the coach park. They informed the police and set off home. In the morning, Mum walked round to where the old lady worked, to tell her employer what had happened, and Auntie Mary opened the door to her.

'I couldn't remember where the coach park was, so I went to the station and caught a train.' she explained. 'I was very lucky, there was one just leaving.'

'Do you realise how much trouble you caused?' Mum asked her.

'Oh, I don't think so.' she said. 'It would have been worse if I'd missed the train.'

Mum said that what annoyed her most, was that they had seen that train leave the station while they were waiting in the coach park.

Auntie Mary became ill and was taken into hospital for an operation to remove gall-stones. This completely unhinged her mind, and they told Mum that it really wasn't safe to let her go back to work, and as she had no other home, she would be better off in an institution. I think they hoped that Mum would take her, but there was no way that Mum could cope with her as well as looking after us. They took her to an institution near Herne Bay, and Mum and I went round to clear out her room. We found drawer after drawer full of bottles - medicine and pill bottles mostly, not alcohol! She must have saved every bottle she ever had. What a pity there was no recycling then.

It was too far away for any of us to go and visit, but Pop still felt a certain responsibility towards her. He went to say with Auntie Bessie for a few days, and decided that it was not too far for him to go from Broadstairs to Herne Bay. When he arrived at the Home, Auntie Mary was out in the garden and he was told to go and find her. This he did, and when she saw him she said,
'What are you doing here?'
'I've come to see you, Mary.'
'Oh, have you,' she said, 'well, it's my tea-time now, so I'm going inside.' and that was the end of that.

When she eventually died, a completely unknown nephew appeared from nowhere and took charge, and possession, of everything.

Then there was Grandma. She wasn't really our grandmother, in fact, she was not related to us at all. When Mum was a little girl, her next-door neighbours had been Mr. and Mrs. Clark and their four children, and it was Mrs. Clark whom we called Grandma. Mum's parents had both died before she herself was married, which I always regretted, as I would have dearly loved to have known her father, whom she adored, and from whom, I believe, I inherited my patience. Anyway, Mrs. Clark took over the position of Grandma and we loved her. She would come to stay at irregular intervals and for irregular lengths of time. She was everyone's idea of a perfect old-fashioned grandma - well padded everywhere, and with an ample bosom just right for a miserable little girl to sob on. She had grey hair with wispy bits always escaping from the bun that was supposed to confine them, and sharp eyes with a permanent twinkle. Everything about her was unhurried. All her movements were slow, and she even spoke slowly, in a throaty sort of voice which matched the gorgeous deep chuckle that seemed to begin way down in her stomach and gradually work its way out. She chuckled a lot. Everything seemed to amuse her, and I can't remember any time when she was irritable or out of temper.

She came to be with Mum when our brother was born. I was seven at the time and Mum was forty-three. As was usual at that time, we children knew nothing about the expected baby until someone told us that we had a baby brother. I don't know whether the birth was straightforward or whether there were complications. Mum had already had one difficult birth - mine, when, as she said, the afterbirth grew to her side, and the doctor couldn't get it away. Anyway, after Eric was born, Grandma took over. She would warm a nappy in front of the fire to put on him, and when he immediately wet it she would give her deep, throaty chuckle and promptly warm another one. Having washed all his soiled nappies, she would then iron them all, the only time any of us had our nappies ironed. She stayed a long time on that occasion, and we were all very sad to see her go.

As she grew older, she came less and less, and, once or twice, I went with Mum to see her when she was staying with her son in Chatham. She died during the war. Mum went down to East Kent for her funeral, and before she left, she asked the local policeman what chance she had of being allowed into the area.
'Very little.' he said.
'But it is the funeral of one of my oldest friends.' she explained.
'Sorry,' he said, 'but that won't cut much ice.'
'Suppose that I say that she was my mother,' she suggested. 'Would they let me in then?'
'Oh yes,' he said 'but you mustn't do that, you know.'
'Well, I will if I need to,' said mum. 'She's been like a mother to me for thirty years since my own mother died, and I am going to be at her funeral.'
She was too.

CHAPTER 9

Pop came from a family of farm labourers in the days when they were regarded as the lowest of the low, and he determined to break free of the land. In the early days of his marriage, he worked on a farm and I can just about remember those days when he cycled two miles to get to work. While I was still very small, he somehow got himself involved in a fish-mongering business, how, I am not sure. He was not very intelligent and had no head for figures and no business sense at all, but he was a very hard worker and a persistent salesman. Mum, who was very intelligent, did all the paperwork. He bought himself a tradesman's bike and went off to collect orders for his fish. The fish came from a firm in Hull, and was sent down to Paddock Wood station every morning, packed in light wooden boxes with crushed ice. We were never short of firewood in those days. On the morning after my brother was born, someone had added 'and son' to his name on the boxes.

Every morning, Pop got up early, lit the fire in the kitchen range, boiled a kettle on the primus stove and another on the oil stove and made tea, which he took up to everyone in bed. He cooked porridge for his breakfast, and then went off to collect his fish. While he was gone, the rest of us got up and had breakfast - which might be bread-and-milk or a basin of cocoa or oxo with bread in it. Sometimes we had fried bread, or what we called dapper, which was bread dipped in beaten egg and fried, but usually we were in too much of a hurry to bother with anything that took too long to prepare. Mum usually had a slice of bread with her homemade marmalade.

The last part of Pop's journey back from the station was up a wicked hill, so I used to run up to the top of the hill and watch for him to come into sight. Then I would run down to meet him and help to push his loaded bike home. Another cup of tea and a chance to get his breath back, and he would be off on his round for the day. One day Mum said to me,
'Don't bother to go and meet Pop this morning, love. I don't think he'll need your help today.' I couldn't believe this, so I went to the top of the hill as usual, just in time to see him chugging up the road on a motor-bike and sidecar. This should have made life much easier for him, but he merely widened his sphere of activity and worked just as hard. In course of time he sold his motor-bike and bought a little car, a Jowett, number KO 5873.

Every evening, he and Mum sat down to do the orders for a few days ahead, which had to be posted off to Hull. They always ordered more than they actually needed in the hope of attracting new customers. We had to be very quiet while this was going on, and the damns came thick and fast if our noise caused them to make a mistake.

Of course, there was often fish left over, sometimes a lot, and, in the days before fridges and freezers, there was only one thing to do with it if it wasn't to be wasted - we had to eat it. We had mountains of fish-cakes for Sunday morning breakfast, shrimps for tea, yellow fish (smoked haddock) for any meal. We had fish pies, kedgeree, home made fish paste, kippers, herrings, sprats - and I have never willingly eaten fish since.

I think the business must have done rather well, because at one point Uncle Frank joined him, and they had two Jowetts on the go, but it all came to an abrupt stop when the war began. From then on, Pop did any job that came to hand. He spent some time working as a woodcutter through the bitterest winter in living memory. During this time, he came home one Friday with his wage packet and was incoherent with rage.
'What do you think that so-and-so did?' he stormed - he never swore indoors. 'He docked me a pound off my money.'
'Didn't you tell him?' Mum asked.
'Of course I did, and do you know what he said?' He said 'Where do you find a labourer earning £5 a week' and I said 'I do, and there'll be a row if I don't get it.'
'Well, did you get it?' she asked.
'He's going to put it right next week.'
When I think about that episode I still feel the same outrage that he did then.

He worked at the wood factory in Paddock Wood and at the canning factory next door to it - not both at the same time. For the latter part of his life he worked as a gardener, and did days or half days in gardens all over the village. For many years, he was the caretaker of the churchyard, and took great pride in keeping it neat and tidy. After he gave up the car, he went everywhere on his bike, getting slower and slower as he got older until we wondered how the thing stayed upright.

When I was in my early twenties I bought him a puppy for his birthday. I was living with Uncle Frank and Auntie Florrie at the time, and their brown spaniel had a litter of four nondescript pups, all very much alike. One had a voice that reminded me of a foghorn, rather like a boy I had in my class at the time named Peter, so I christened the pup Foghorn Peter, and that was the one I took home to Pop. At first it was called Foggy but, not surprisingly, Pop didn't like that, and kept thinking of other names for him, but he was called Peter to the end of his very long life. The two of them were inseparable. When Pop was walking, Peter was about five yards ahead, and when Pop was cycling, Peter ran alongside. He would always bark excitedly when they first went out of the door, and keep it up for just too long. Pop would get on his bicycle and yell,
'Stop that silly noise.' The dog would take no notice at all and Pop would repeat the command several times. Finally, he would take off his cap and throw it at the dog, who would ignore it completely, but Pop would have to get off the bike and retrieve his cap and get back on again, by which time the dog had given up barking and was ready to go. The routine never varied and we always found it highly amusing.

Actually, we were amused by much that Pop did. He didn't share our kind of humour, and often complained that he didn't know what we were laughing at, which made us laugh all the more. His humour was strictly of the slapstick variety, and anything more subtle escaped him completely. It didn't help that very often we could laugh till we ached without actually making a sound, and he didn't realise that we were laughing for quite some time. He couldn't bear us laughing at him, but it was impossible not to.

He was the only person I ever met who ate soup with a knife and fork. He enjoyed a bowl of soup, but he wasn't pleased when Mum served soup as a starter. He complained that it ruined his appetite, and couldn't understand why we laughed. His method of consuming his soup was to put a whole slice of bread into the soup-plate, so that it became saturated, and then eat it with a knife and fork. He reckoned that using a spoon was only for babies.

He was more accident-prone than anyone I have ever known. One evening, a soldier knocked at the door and asked the way to Wadhurst. He was hoping to catch a bus, but there wasn't a bus service to Wadhurst. He had already walked more than two miles from the station, and had at least another ten to go. Pop pointed him in the right direction, and came in, but he wasn't happy.

'It'll be dark long before he gets to Wadhurst,' he said, 'and it's all country roads and no lights. I wish I'd offered him a bed for the night and let him go on in the morning.'

A few minutes later he put down his book - he only ever read westerns - and said,

'I'm going after him. He can't have got far.' So he got out his bike, left Peter at home, and went off down the hill. When he got to the village, a car came across his path at the junction, and knocked him off his bike. He finished up perched on the bonnet of the car. Neither he nor his bike were badly hurt, and were brought home by the motorist, who professed his willingness to do anything to make amends. Pop was beside himself with rage, but Mum's first thoughts were with the unknown soldier.

'Just think,' she said, 'he's still walking on to Wadhurst, and he'll never know how much trouble you got into, trying to help him.'

Another time he was very worried because his adored eldest daughter, now married with two little children and another on the way, was living in a farm cottage along a narrow lane. There had been a heavy fall of snow and she had very little coal. He was sure that the coal lorry would never even attempt to get up that lane, so, as we had a good stock, he decided to take her some of ours. He filled a sack, tied it securely (?) on to the carrier of his bike and set out. He rode where he could, but most of the time he had to walk, as the roads were slippery and dangerous. He had just turned into her lane, when a car came towards him. There wasn't room for both of them and in trying to get out of the way, Pop, his bicycle and the sack of coal fell into the ditch. It goes without saying that the sack burst open and the coal fell out. Mum said, that to finish the story in style, the coal lorry ought to have come past at that moment on its way to deliver her coal - but it didn't.

Pop was an inveterate collector - mainly of things that wouldn't go and he thought he could fix. One of his treasured possessions was a black marble clock, which he managed to get going. Unfortunately it stopped, but he liked it so much that he took it to a local clock-mender and actually paid to have it repaired. On the day that he collected it, he decided to call and see his grandchildren on the way home. As he walked up their garden path, his son-in-law came rushing out on his bicycle, obviously in a bit of a rage, and knocked Pop and his precious clock into a flower border. Luckily the clock survived. Several years after his death, the clock played up again and my brother had a go at mending it. He replaced it on to the mantelpiece at about twenty to eleven and went to bed. At eleven o'clock it began to strike and all three of us, Eric, Mum and I, listened with bated breath to see how many it would strike. It struck 366.

After Pop's death, Peter attached himself to Mum, and became exclusively hers. He protected her at all times, and obviously had no intention of losing her too. He became very deaf and almost blind, and when anyone came to see Mum, he would get between the two of them and stare fixedly up into the face of the visitor. Many people found this very disconcerting, and the doctor for one found it very inconvenient. It wasn't easy trying to take her pulse, her temperature or blood-pressure with a dog sitting firmly between the two of them. Luckily the doctor understood and would say,
'It's alright, Peter, I'm not going to hurt her.' His name was Peter too.

Peter got to the stage when he was quite deaf, quite blind and unable to walk or even stand properly, so we decided that his quality of life was so minimal that we sent for an RSPCA representative to come and put him down. He agreed to come at 11 o'clock the next day, but at 10.30 precisely, Peter, who was lying on the mat in front of the fire, took matters into his own paws and quietly passed away. He was 16 years old.

When we were small, before the war, Mum very seldom left the house except to go to work. In fact she had a very poor opinion of people who were 'always out' and wondered how they got their housework done. The conclusion was that they didn't. Everything possible was delivered, so there was no need for her to go shopping on a regular basis, but every so often things caught up with her, and she found it necessary to Go Into Tunbridge Wells - I use the capitals deliberately! This was a chore that she hated. It was planned well ahead, and she knew exactly what she was going to buy. If any of us needed new clothes that were out of her power to make, then we were taken with her, otherwise we were left at home with Pop. At 2.15, she would catch the small single-decker bus that stopped outside the house, and she would return at 5.45. If things didn't go as planned, and she had to use the double-decker that went through the village and walk up the hill, she was furious.

We used to beg to be taken with her, but it was no fun if we were. She would buy exactly what she went for, and nothing else. She went swiftly from shop to shop, knowing precisely which was the best one for everything she needed. We never had any money to spend, and she never bought us anything frivolous, so it was merely the change of scene that was exciting. It may sound hard to modern children that she never bought us little presents, but she never had done so, and we didn't expect anything or look for it so we never felt deprived. When any little windfalls did come our way, we appreciated them much more than today's children appreciate anything. Once again, my acute travel-sickness made me an embarrassment so she didn't take me with her if should possibly avoid it. There was also the undeniable fact that I tended to get lost.

In those days, Marks and Spencers was a most boring place for a tiny girl. The counters on which goods were displayed were way above my head, and all I could see was the wooden panelling on which they were based. I could not understand why mum wanted to stand for so long by a wall of wood. I tried to see patterns in the grain of the wood, twisting my head this way and that, and all but standing on my head. One day, when I stood upright again Mum wasn't there. I was sure she hadn't gone far, so I trotted to the end of the counter and looked down the next aisle. I couldn't see very well so I went along it to have a closer look. At last I saw her grey raincoat, so I went to her and pulled her skirt. I was rather distressed that she completely ignored me, and tugged harder. To my horror, a perfectly strange lady looked down at me. I opened my mouth to yell, but before I could do so, my big sister appeared and, grabbing me by the arm, dragged me back to Mum, berating me all the way for causing her so much bother. I'm not really surprised that Mum preferred to leave me at home!

Now and again, when she couldn't help herself, Mum would buy little things from the village shops, but things were so much more expensive there that she hated doing it. Then she would send one of us down to the village - usually me, because I was placid and didn't moan - and sometimes, very rarely, would allow us to spend a penny on ourselves. You could get quite a lot for a penny. The first time I ever had pocket money was when I started at the grammar school. Then I was allowed a shilling a week and I felt really wealthy. I never spent it all, and saved enough to buy little birthday presents for the rest of the family. I bought peanuts once a week.

Unsalted ones were exactly half the price of the salted variety, and I could never decide whether to go for quantity or quality, though actually I liked them both. The others always helped to eat them, so it paid to get unsalted ones.

On very rare occasions, we found it necessary to go somewhere by train - to an aunt in Broadstairs or another one in Ramsgate or to Mum's childhood friends in Sturry or Canterbury. While Pop had his little car it wasn't too bad. He never came with us, and would take us to the station and collect us when we returned. However, when the car was no more, it was a different story. We then had to walk to Paddock Wood or, at times, Mum would send us off early to walk, and would follow later on her bike, which she would leave at the station ready for her return. This practice had certain inherent flaws, mainly the fact that we were country children and quite incapable of walking by a grassy bank when we could be on it, of by-passing a possible bird's nest without investigating it or missing a chance to find wild strawberries, primroses or violets, thereby making an hour's journey last at least two. The return journey, when we were all tired, was murder.

When I was a very little girl, my parents became concerned about the fact that I always held my reading book too close to my face, added to which I blinked a lot. Instead of coming to the obvious conclusion, they kept pulling my book away and slapping my hands. They sent a note to school asking the teachers to slap me every time I blinked. I remember hearing Miss Trill saying to my class teacher,
'I can't do that and neither can you.' I have no idea who decided to have my eyes tested, but for a year or two, Mum had to take me, at three-monthly intervals to a clinic in Tonbridge. It meant the walk to Paddock Wood, a ride on a train to Tonbridge and then a fairly long walk the other end. They always said there was nothing wrong, but they'd better keep an eye on me.

One day it was very hot, and Pop was planning to meet us with the car at 3.30. As luck would have it, we got away from the clinic early and were in Paddock Wood by 2 pm. Mum didn't want to sit and wait for an hour and a half so we began to walk. Mum hated the heat, and the long drag uphill in the afternoon sun was almost more than she could take. Little as I was - about nine, I reckon, I tried to space myself so that at least some of my shadow fell on her and spared her a bit of the sun. I realise now that it was futile, but she was deeply grateful for the attempt.

Just to complete the day, when we were safely home, she told me to wait outside, and when I saw the car to be sure and let Pop see me, and stop him from going to the station to meet us. I saw him coming and I stood by the side of the road and waved. He took no notice of me whatsoever and went straight on to the station.

After many years of trailing to and from Tonbridge, the people at the clinic told Mum that really there was nothing wrong with my eyes, and even suggested that I had been pretending because I fancied myself in glasses. It wasn't until I had a medical at the end of my college years that it was discovered how acutely short-sighted I was, and arrangements were made for me to have glasses right away. I was absolutely amazed at the difference it made to me. I could actually read the numbers on the hymn-board in church - I had always wondered what use they were if no-one could see them clearly! I could see things on the other side of the room and nothing was blurred. I had never dreamed that sight could be like that.

The only other things that caught the interest of the doctor at that college medical were my vaccination scars. All three of us, as babies, were vaccinated on our upper arms by an old doctor, who had very shaky hands, and our scars are enormous. The four white marks grew as we grew, and mine are now each at least an inch in diameter, and, although the rest of me goes brown in the sun, they don't. People have often said to me, that in my place they would always keep them covered, but they never worry me and I am not in the least self-conscious about them. I've been vaccinated once or twice since then, and the doctors have been very careful to place the new marks inside the old ones so they are completely lost.

I can remember very clearly when we first acquired our own wheels. We were sent into the pantry on Christmas morning, and there were two green scooters. Very basic they were, but we loved them and were seldom seen out without them. The exhilaration of zimming down the hills with both feet on the footplate was well worth the slog of pushing them back up again. Nellie had a bike that year but we weren't in the least jealous. Mum had a 'sit-up-and-beg' bike, and I learned to ride on that. I used to meet her as she came home from work, commandeer her bike and try to ride it. I could get nowhere near the saddle, but I used to stand on the pedals and count how many times I could turn them round before I fell off - it was a long time before I could even honestly count one. As it was all uphill, it was a very hard task I had set myself, but in the end persistence paid off, and I managed to ride several yards without mishap.

In the fullness of time Nellie bought Auntie Mary's bike - which was a wonderful machine, as it had a three-speed lever which helped when going uphill, as she was never tired of pointing out - and I inherited her bike. I can't remember a time when we actually had a bike each, but there were usually enough for anyone who wanted to ride one. It was wonderful to be mobile, and there were occasions when I cycled all the way into Tunbridge Wells to school.

Very early on in the war I joined the Junior Red Cross, and spent every Thursday evening, in one of the back rooms of the hall, learning how to do bandaging and anything else that might be of use in the event of an invasion or any other emergency. I detested the choice of evening as it kept me away from one of the regular whist drives, but apart from that I quite enjoyed it. There were about six of us, and we took exams and were awarded badges. I always got top marks, sometimes 100%, mainly because much of the work was learning anatomy, and I had done all that at school.

We prided ourselves that we were becoming really useful members of the community, able to cope with anything in the realms of first aid. One summer evening, as two of us were walking home together, we passed by a dog that was sniffing away quite harmlessly on the grass verge. A few yards further on, just round a corner, we met one of the local teenage tearaways on his bike, racing along almost out of control. As he rounded the corner out of our sight, there was a sudden outbreak of frenzied barking, a clatter of metal and the sound of furious swearing. Then there was an ominous silence. We looked at each other in horror and, without saying a word, we ran as fast as we could in the opposite direction. We learned afterwards that the silence was because he had successfully kicked the dog away and continued on his way. So much for coping!

94

The lady who taught us sustained a visit from an American aunt, and thought we would like to hear what she had to tell us about life in the New World. On this occasion, we went to her home and sat on dining chairs lined up in her sitting room. After a little while, the two ladies realised that no-one was really paying attention to what was being said, and the speaker began to struggle. Actually we were all watching a huge spider, that was walking, in erratic little spurts, along the top of the wall behind them. Finally, when she realised that her aunt had lost us completely, our teacher asked me what was taking our attention, and I told her. The effect was unexpected, amazing and utterly hilarious. The aunt leapt on a chair, flailing her arms around her, and screamed,

'No, no, get it away. Don't let it come near me. Where is it?' and then she hugged her arms round her body and sobbed.

At first we watched in silent disbelief, but then the giggles took over, and we collapsed helplessly on to our chairs. When she remembered that she was in England, she came down from the chair, and explained to us about the deadly poisonous black widow spider of America. She was completely unable to continue with her talk, so all we learned that evening was the life style of the black widow.

At one point it was decided that, to help the war effort, the Junior Red Cross Unit was to grow onions. Our teacher acquired a patch of ground near her home, and told us all to meet there instead of at the hall. It was a two mile walk for most of us, and we were less than enthusiastic about it all. We were allotted one row between two, and she said to me,

'I've put you to share a row with Donald. Is that alright?'

Donald's well-deserved nickname was Goopy and I was not very pleased.

'I don't mind.' I said.

'Well is that what you want?' she persisted. 'Donald told me that you said you wanted to be his partner.' Cheeky monkey! It didn't make a lot of difference anyway. I can't remember going up there more than a couple of times, and I never saw an onion.

Another time we all went down to the Fire Station in Paddock Wood, which, for the duration of the war, was an air-raid centre, to learn how to put out a fire using a stirrup pump. We were told all the commands and the positions of the team, and then a controlled fire was lit for us to extinguish.

Nearby, there was a row of buckets filled with water, and when someone shouted 'fire' we ran to our correct positions - one of us manning the pump, one directing the nozzle, one fetching buckets of water and so on. On the command 'Water on.' the pumper started pumping and the fire was successfully doused. Then we were to change places and repeat the performance. The fireman tossed the rest of the straw into the bay, and went off with two of the buckets to refill them. Unfortunately the previous nozzle holder had shouted 'Water off.' a bit too soon and a few sparks remained. Suddenly the straw went up in flames.

'This will be good practice,' called out our teacher. 'You can put this fire out.' The boys did just that. They each grabbed a bucket, and threw its contents on to the burning straw. So, there being no more straw, that was the end of that.

Another bright idea for making use of the Junior Red Cross members, came about because a well-known London hospital had evacuated its maternity unit to a large mansion on the outskirts of the village, and they thought we would like to spend the occasional Sunday afternoon helping with the babies. We went down in twos, but we weren't allowed anywhere near the babies. We made mounds of sandwiches for the patients' teas, laid out miles of cups and saucers and stacked up mountains of dirty crocks. On one occasion, something had gone wrong with the water supply, and we spent the whole afternoon working an antique pump to fill up a water tank. Our arms ached, our backs ached, our hands were covered in blisters and I thought longingly of the front room fire at home.

After a while, most of the others began to find really good reasons for not taking their turn, and I found myself going every other week. By this time, I was allowed to help with changing the babies' nappies, but it was too late. I'd had enough. The loss of my Sunday afternoons at home proved too much for me, and I found reasons for staying there. The whole scheme then folded.

My Tuesday evenings were spent at a Country Dance club, which was held in the big infants classroom at the village school. There was an elderly lady living on the outskirts of the village, who took classes in several villages around, mainly for adults but she was happy to include selected children.

We did dancing at school, but only when it rained during our normal games period. Half of us had indoor games in the gym and the other half had country dancing in the hall. I can't remember that we actually had a choice. We went where we were instructed to go. As these lessons occurred rather infrequently, we seemed to spend all our time learning Flowers of Edinburgh and Bonnets so Blue. Most of the girls never mastered the concept of a duple minor set, and set dances of two, three or four couples were obviously considered way beyond us. I doubt very much if our teacher had ever heard of a triple minor formation.

Our Tuesday evening classes were quite different. To start with of course, everyone was there because they wanted to dance, and we children were pushed and pulled, in a very good-natured fashion, until we knew how to be in the right place at the right time. We learned really complicated set dances and their intricate patterns fascinated me. It began what was to be a lifetime interest. I went on to join a club at college, which organised frequent trips to Cecil Sharpe House, and after that I joined another class with my old teacher. She took me to dance with other teams, and we frequently gave displays at fetes and garden parties. Later still I had classes of my own.

CHAPTER 10

One of the absolute highlights of the year for us, was the Flower Show, which occurred at the end of July. We children weren't in the least interested in the exhibits of fruit, flowers, vegetables and what-have-you. Oh no! we went because of Tommy Andrews' Fair. Swing-boats, coconut-shies, roundabouts - the old kind, with horses on golden spiral rods that went up and down as you went round on them - roll-a-penny, rifle range, bumper-cars and all sorts of other side shows, we never knew from one year to the next what delights would be there.

The excitement began on the day before the actual show, because, on our way home from school, we would see the tents and booths being erected. In fact, sometimes, from our classroom windows, we had watched them come along the road, and lessons might just as well have stopped right there! Mum was well aware of the temptation, and we were forbidden to enter the show field on the Friday night. The punishment for disobedience was no money to spend next day, and the risks were too high. We all knew that Mum had eyes everywhere, and that we had no chance whatsoever of going into that field without being found out, so, reluctantly, we went straight home.

Soon after dinner on the Saturday, the hurdy-gurdy would start up, and from then on the music would torture us until Mum said we could go. She usually let us go just before two o'clock, and she gave us each 6d to spend. In those days, the rides and booths cost 1d or 2d a go, and if we were careful and wise we could win a few extra pennies to eke the 6d out.

There was always a display of our school work in the marquee - handwriting, pictures, needlework and so on - and also a wild flower competition, which was won by the person with the greatest variety of flowers in their jam-jar. Pop used to take us out around the wilder parts of the village in his little Jowett, so that we could find as many different flowers as possible. We almost always won several prizes, and as the three of us came into different age groups, we never competed against each other.

There were also races, flat, egg-and-spoon, three-legged, obstacle, skipping and all the other old favourites. I wasn't so overweight in my younger days, and could run with the best of them. I also acquired the knack of keeping a china egg on a spoon and once again, we nearly always won a few shillings. The unfortunate thing was that these prizes were not handed out till later on, so they weren't much good to us during the afternoon.

Mum and Pop and anyone else who happened to be around used to come down about six to see the exhibits, and watch the prizes being given. If we could show Mum that we still had some of our money left, then she would give us a little more, but if we had spent out that was that. She herself enjoyed the roll-a-penny board, and she would set aside so much and when it was gone, she stopped. She figured there was no way they could cheat you on that, as long as you kept your eyes firmly on the coins you rolled.

I always wanted to win a coconut but, as my aim was, and still is, shall we say, erratic? I was doomed to failure, but, by hook or by crook, we usually ended the day with two or three of the things. Needless to say, like so many other things, coconuts now just don't seem to taste the same somehow.

I loved the swing-boats, which was a pity really as they invariably made me sick. There were child-sized ones and big ones, and many of the more daring children went on the adult ones. I envied them enormously, especially when they swung their boats almost over the top bar, but I stuck to the juvenile size and even then I was, or felt, sick. Come to think of it, that was one way of making my money last out as, while I was battling with the after-effects of the swing-boats, I just sat down in a corner and didn't want to have a go on anything.

The roundabout I simply adored - and I still do. The sight of those horses going up-and-down on their spiral rods can bring on nostalgia like nothing else can - even if it's only in a Peter Sellers film.

Quite often there were chairoplanes - a huge construction that whirled round and sent its chairs flying round in space. There wasn't anything in heaven or on earth that would get me on one of those.

By the time that Mum shepherded us all home, we were almost too tired to walk up the hill, and the music that followed us all the way was no longer mocking us, but providing a background to the end of a perfect day.

As the Flower Show was always on the same Saturday each year, people who had left the village would often come back for the occasion, and be sure of meeting old friends. It was a great social occasion, and we children were quite likely to be slipped the odd few pence by someone we hadn't seen for a year.

As the afternoon drew into evening, the rides would be taken by the young men and women - upper teenagers and twenties who were earning their own money and could afford to indulge themselves. Then the rides were shorter, as the operators tried to cope with the number of punters, and any children left around were very much in the way.

We went to sleep to the sound of the hurdy-gurdy, and by the time we next went by the field, it was all packed up and gone - or ready to go. A few years ago, walking round that field with the dog, I met a man with a metal detector. He told me that he had heard that the fair used to be held there, and he had hopes of finding some money. He needn't have bothered. On the day after the Flower Show, the boys descended in droves onto the field, and went over it more thoroughly than any metal detector. By the time the boys gave up, you could be absolutely sure that there was not so much as a farthing lurking in the grass.

The tail-end of the Flower show, of course, was at school on the following Monday when we had to write about it. We took care to mention every ride we had been on and every side-show we had patronised, and tried to get them in the correct order.

We had several more weeks of school after the show, as we didn't break up for the long holiday until the third week in August. That was the hop-picking holiday, and we went back to school during the first week in October.

During those last few weeks at school the hop-pickers arrived from London's East End, and took up residence in the hop-huts. These were erected, in ranks of eight to twelve, somewhere near the hop-garden, each one being a wooden hut about ten foot square, with a bed-shaped structure along one side. The occupants found straw to put on this, and brought some bed-clothes with them. All cooking was done over a huge communal fire, which was fed with faggots of brushwood from under the haystacks.

Some of the children came to school for a week or so, but their London schools broke up before we did, and once that had happened they didn't come any more. They were so different from us country children. Their values and priorities were not the same as ours, and as hardly any of us had ever been to London, they could get away with the tallest stories imaginable. On the whole we despised them, and as we never really had time to get to know them better, we were glad when they went back home and left our village to us.

Years later, I had a teaching job at the Elephant and Castle, and saw these people from the other side, as it were. I soon learned how warm-hearted they are and found that, if they accepted you, there was nothing they wouldn't do for you. For many poor families, the weeks spent in the country 'darn 'oppin' ' were the nearest thing to a holiday they were ever likely to get. To them 'Oppin was a place. That was its name. Nevertheless, when the hop-pickers arrived, all the village shops covered the front of their counters with wire netting, and removed all their goods behind it. It was bonanza time for the shop-keepers, just as long as they could make sure that money actually changed hands for all the goods that left the shop.

The pubs, of course, did a roaring trade. The bars would be full, and crowds would be standing outside unable to get in. Every night the singing would start as soon as they left the pubs - they had usually got to 'Nellie Dean' by the time they went past us. Mum reckoned that they made so much noise because they were afraid of the dark in a place where there were no street lights.

They appeared to think of 'the country' as a place where nothing happened or was likely to happen, therefore they treated the roads like footpaths. Crowds of them - they always moved in crowds - would sprawl across the road, taking up the whole width of it, completely ignoring any traffic that chanced to come along. Why they weren't killed in droves is a mystery.

To see a hopper's train come into the station at Paddock Wood, was as good as a pantomime. Everything would be quiet and peaceful, not a porter in sight, as the little train slipped under the bridge and alongside the platform. Suddenly all hell would break loose. The train literally exploded, with people shooting out like seeds out of a seedpod. Porters appeared from nowhere and shepherded them, just like a flock of unruly sheep, up the steps and over the footbridge to where the farm lorries were waiting for them, skilfully fielding small boys away from anything portable before it disappeared. The noise was deafening. Then the lorries drove off, the train steamed away and the station went to sleep again until the next one came.

During hop-picking, it was virtually impossible to get on a Tunbridge Wells bus on a Saturday afternoon. The buses that came past our house, finished their outward run two miles down the road, and the afternoon bus would be packed to the doors before it began the return journey. Mum tried to avoid any trips into town, until hopping was over and things returned to normal, but if circumstances made it absolutely essential, she would catch the bus as it came by on its outward run, and remain on it while it turned round. Sometimes the bus crew was difficult and made one get off and wait in turn with the seething crowds outside, but most of them, being locals themselves, were fully in sympathy with the seasonal difficulties that local people had to put up with.

Those little buses were a real asset to the area. The timetable hardly varied from year to year, and we all knew it by heart. Most of the drivers were, or became, friends of ours, and could be relied on to stop the bus exactly where we wanted to get off. One of them used to sing to his passengers all the way home, and it was not unknown, on a wet night, for the bus to make a slight detour or two, so that one or another of the regular passengers could be dropped right on their doorstep instead of having a ten-minute walk. The fare was a penny a mile. Many a time Mum set one or another of us to stand outside, wait for the bus and stop it when it came, so that she could nip out at the last minute and get on it. The drivers never seemed to mind.

They had to make a detour anyway when the roads were being re-surfaced. We were highly excited when that happened. The funny little copper-like things on wheels, that held and heated the tar, would arrive first, then the men with the grit lorry and the steam roller. Melted tar would be released from the back end of the tar boiler, and smoothed over the road by men wielding paddle like things - rather like rakes without any prongs. Then the grit lorry would deposit a load of grit, which would also be evened out by the men with their paddles. Finally came the steam roller - a really majestic machine, that chugged up and down along the newly gritted stretch of road, until the surface was flat and all the grit-stones were absorbed into the tar. It took several days for our stretch of the road to be finished, and we were quite happy just to stand and watch.

When the excitement was all over, we looked for tar bubbles to pop - we learned very early the unwisdom of trying to emulate Brer Rabbit and make tar babies. Mum wasn't amused.

By the time the war ended, I was in my last year at the Grammar School, and it was only then that we realised what we had missed because of it. We had no trips abroad as school parties, no foreign pen-friends to exchange visits with, no trips to London theatres to see performances of plays that we were studying, and no activities of any kind on Saturdays, or that involved the use of petrol. Exercise books had to be used to the very last centimetre, and books for rough work were filled up in pencil and then used again in ink.

Many of our lessons were interrupted by frantic dashes to the trenches when the air raid siren sounded, and although the teachers strove manfully to keep going, the lighting was insufficient, and as we sat on narrow benches and had no desks, written work was impossible. It was also well-nigh impossible to hear anything that was said by someone sitting at the other end of the line of benches, and often it was easier to hear the lesson that was going on in the next arm of the trench.

School uniform was not expected to be affected by clothes rationing.
'If you need a new coat girls, what colour must it be? That's right, navy blue. New shoes? Brown of course. Use your clothing coupons for school uniform before anything else.' Only many girls didn't.

During my second year, whilst schooling was still part-time, I was summoned to the Headmistress's study. My knees knocked as I tapped on the door. She was a very gentle sort of person, who never raised her voice but could reduce a whole hall full of girls to jelly by saying, sadly,

'Girls, I am very disappointed......'

She tended to call us all 'Old Lady' when she wasn't cross, so when she said to me,

'Come and sit down, Old Lady.' I felt a bit better! She shuffled a few papers around and then said,

'Your school dinners are paid for by the County, are they not?'

'Y-y-yes.' I stammered.

'Then why aren't you having them?'

'I have to catch a bus home when we have a morning session, and when I come in for the afternoon, I don't get here in time.'

'Rubbish! Catch an earlier bus in and a later one out. Your mother doesn't want to feed you every day when your dinners are paid for here. Food is rationed you know.' And that was that!

The time came when we were all summoned to her study to discuss our future careers. When it was my turn, I remembered my vow of years ago, 'When I grow up I'm going to be a teacher, then I'll be able to hit kids.' So I said to her,

'I've always wanted to be a teacher, but now I realise that I'm not good enough at any one subject to be able to teach it.'

'Nonsense, old lady.' she replied, 'You don't have to be a specialist. The primary school is the place for you. You'll make a lovely little teacher.'

Forgetting the word little, I hope, in the past 40 years, I have come up to her expectations.

I knew nothing of training colleges, and I chose Furzedown, halfway between Tooting and Streatham, in order to be with one of my friends. I may add that she did not remain my friend after our first year there.

It meant an interview in County Hall, Westminster, where the College Principal confided that her niece had attended our school. I was greener than grass in those days, and completely unable to get myself to London and find my way around. After all, during the war, it was impossible to go there, and I had never in my life been in London, so Uncle Frank and Auntie Florrie were co-erced into taking me - in a snowstorm.

104

The college had been evacuated to Cardiff during the war, and the buildings had suffered a certain amount of damage, so when it was time for us to begin our training, we couldn't. At first we were told to go to a local school and lend a hand, so I went to the school where my brother was a pupil. I was there for two or three weeks, and during that time, a lecturer came down from college to look me over. The class teacher I was with was a darling, and the day before the visit, she suggested that we take the children out for a walk, to collect some nature specimens which I could use as the basis for a lesson.

As the time drew near for the lecturer's arrival, I made sure that everything was ready, so that I could launch into my prepared lesson as soon as she appeared - and not before. Having had to send explicit instructions as to how to find me, I knew which bus she'd be on, but it went right past the school without stopping. We waited another 45 minutes, and it was getting dangerously near to home time when she finally appeared. She was the ugliest person I have ever seen, with a face just like a camel, but, as I was to learn, was loved by everyone for her wonderful nature.

'I am so sorry my dear,' she said to me, 'but I missed the school and was taken on to the village. It's the loveliest place I have ever seen, and there was no way I could leave without going in to that beautiful church. What a wonderful place to live in.' Whenever we met in college in the next two years she always said,

'Ah, yes. You're the one who lives in that beautiful village in Kent.'

For the rest of that Autumn term, we were told to get ourselves jobs as uncertificated teachers, and I was sent to a school in Tonbridge. I can say, without the shadow of a doubt, that that was the most miserable period of my life. The headmistress was a bitch of the first water. She treated all her staff badly, but she went to town on me. The office sent her a letter, saying how much I was to be paid, and she told me that she had replied saying I wasn't worth it. She did her damnedest every evening to make me miss my bus home, so that I had an hour to wait, and didn't get home till well after six, when school had finished at 3.45. The children feared and loathed her and the staff despised and loathed her. When the children had their Christmas party she found me, with the other teachers, helping and joining in with the children's games, and she shouted at me,

'You shouldn't be here, get in the kitchen and do the washing up.' On the last day of that term I went home and cried my eyes out.

College came as a revelation, a completely new way of life. To begin with we were all called Miss....., never a Christian name. I was situated in the newest of the hostels, called Cedars, and my room was on the top floor. We were only allowed to use the lift on the first and last days of term, when we would have heavy bags to carry. Our rooms were light and airy and contained a bed, a desk and chair, a bookcase and an armchair. A square carpet covered the middle of the floor, and there were two lights, one in the centre of the ceiling and one over the desk. The built-in wardrobe, with a set of drawers in the same fitment, gave ample room for clothes, and the room was heated by an effective radiator. There was a general purposes room on each floor and several bathrooms and washing cubicles. On the ground floor were the dining room, the lounge and several small rooms for entertaining visitors, who were not allowed in our own rooms. There were three hostels, and all other students were billeted out in the neighbourhood.

Food was still rationed, and every week we had to put our containers on the trolley in the dining room, to receive our personal ration of butter and margarine. All other rations were used in the kitchens to prepare our main meals. We were expected to help with the washing up at tea-time, and there was a rota for so doing.

We were expected to be in by 10 pm. when the outer doors were locked. There was a floor representative on each floor, who had to take the ten o'clock book, signed by all the girls, down to the duty warden. We were allowed to stay out till midnight for special reasons, and no tabs were kept on us. To do that, we had to sign the late book, and report on our return to whichever warden was on late duty, who could be in any one of the hostels. I was very much the country girl when I arrived at college, and I took a long time to settle in. I missed my home and family and the non-stop chatter I was used to. I missed the freedom of country lanes and fields to wander in. I felt smothered by city streets, shops, buses and trams and I felt I would never get to know any of the girls, who all seemed to be much more confident than I was. If only I had known! After a few weeks, I became one of a group who stuck together for the rest of the two years. I joined the Folk Dance society which met every Friday evening, and found that I knew more dances than most of the other members. I also joined the Christian Union.

During my final teaching practice, in January 1947, we had the bitterest weather and the heaviest snowfalls for years, and everyone in college went down with 'flu.' Sister had all her beds in 'san' filled with patients, and she was nursing about thirty others in their own rooms. I went over to her surgery because I had a sore throat, and was admitted right away with tonsillitis. Sister was overjoyed to have a patient with something other than 'flu,' and she fussed over me like an old hen. When I felt well enough, I spent my time doing crosswords and jig-saw puzzles, and she always stopped by my bed to solve a clue or put a few bits of a puzzle in place. Like me, she was an addict. She was a fiery Scotswoman, and she would berate us all on any subject, from how to make our beds properly to having our bath water too hot, but she always made an exception of me. She called me 'my poor lassie' and insisted that I was the only one who was really ill. M&B tablets were the very newest drugs and I had to suck them. They were big, like peppermints, and as you sucked the shell away they became covered in a sticky jelly-like substance, which tasted horrible.

One morning, Principal came in with some very official-looking visitors. Sister got into the ward first, whipped away my crossword book and pushed me under the clothes.
'Now you just lie there and look ill' she hissed, 'and leave the rest to me.'

Apparently, the visitors were there to check up on sick students who were not completing their final school practice, to see if they should be made to start it all over again. Several of them did have to.

When they came over to me, I smiled wanly at them and Principal said,
'Now this one has been very poorly indeed. Sister has been really worried about her.' Had she? Sister said,
'She couldn't have used her voice at all. She was quite unable to speak - and her temperature....' She showed them my chart and they all nodded wisely. I attempted to sit up, but Principal gently pushed me back and said,
'No dear, just lie still and get well. I am sure you'll feel better soon.' They all murmured agreement and that was the end of that. Sister gave me the thumbs-up sign behind their backs, and I heard no more about making up my school practice.

Before we left college for the great big world, we had a medical. The first things the doctor noticed were my vaccination marks and called everyone handy to come and take a look at them. Then he tested my eyes and tut-tutted like mad. He asked about my previous eye history, and when I told him about my regular visits to Tonbridge and the final outcome he almost exploded.

'Silly lot of fools!' he raged 'You are painfully short-sighted. Do you get head-aches? Yes, I thought so. Good heavens, studying must have been hell for you.'

He arranged for me to go to Moorfields, so that I could be fitted with spectacles before I stopped being a student, and so get them free. That just about wrapped up my medical.

And so I left college to take my place in the adult world. But that's another story!